BACK FROM BROKEN....

A DANCERS JOURNEY BACK TO WHOLENESS

ROSHEKA HENRY

Arlena Dean,
Thank you So much
for reviewing my
book. I hope it's a
blessing to you. May
God bless you.
Rosheka
Henry

JNF ENTERPRISES
BALTIMORE, MARYLAND

First Published by JNF Enterprises 6/2016

Back From Broken....A Dancers Journey Back To
Wholeness: By Rosheka Henry

ISBN 978-0-692-73455-1

Library of Congress Cataloging –in-Publication Data

Cover Design by NV Graphic Design

TABLE OF CONTENTS

DEDICATION

This book is dedicated to my children, Moriah, Maya, and Cade. I am so blessed that God entrusted me to be your mother. To my parents, Pastor John and Darlene Cook. Thank you for introducing me to Jesus Christ, and for all the love and sacrifices you've made for our family. To my sisters Jennifer and Melanie, I love you all so much. Thank you for not only being my sisters but my friends. To all the family and friends who have supported me on this journey, thank you for believing in me. I love you all dearly. Most importantly, I'd like to thank my Lord and Savior, Jesus Christ for making this book possible, and for carrying me on this hour.

Rosheka S. Henry

ACKNOWLEDGEMENTS

Giving all the glory and the honor to Jesus Christ who is truly the head of my life. There is nothing that I can do without Him, and there isn't anything that I can't do with Him.

I'd like to honor my daddy/pastor John L. Cook Jr. and my mother/elect lady Darlene Cook for being there for me when I got it wrong, and when I got it right. Thank you for every sacrifice you've made for me and my children. Often times we don't understand what we have until it's gone. Please know that I am so blessed to have you in my life. I couldn't have asked God for better parents. You have fought the good fight of faith. I have witnessed it. You have watched over my soul as a pastor and elect lady, and I've seen you do the same for others. Your labor will not be in vain. I love you both dearly. You are my heroes.

To my darling children. Moriah, Maya, and Cade. My love for you only grows more and more each day. You have been there through the tough times. But God has graced us with His mercy time and time again. Whatever you do in life, you must keep God first, or it will fail. He is the source of your strength. Do not let this world tell you anything different. Always look to the hills from whence cometh your help. All your help comes from the Lord. He is your Alpha and Omega, beginning and end. Stay focused and remember, Jesus + education = success. Love everyone, even your enemies with all of your hearts. Forgive those who may hurt you. Do not hold on to anger and bitterness my loves. Let it go! Most of all, remember, this earth is not your home, you are just passing through. Heaven is your final destination if you love God and keep His commandments. Love, Mom

To my sisters Jennifer and Melanie, Thank you for your love and support. Thank you for all that you do to make our family one of love and happiness. I have learned so much from both of you even though I am the oldest. You two are the most wonderful sisters that I could ask for. Thank you for all of my nieces and nephews. I love them so much. It's a blessing to have sisters that you can call on for prayer at any given time. Sisters that have your back no matter what storm may come my way. Thank you because I can always count on you two. I love you.

To my Word of Truth Ministries family, I love you all so much. Thank you for loving me. You are my family. Thank you for the good times, and thank you for the hard times that we have overcome together. Thank you to those parents and grandparents who have trusted me with hours of practice with their children. I am honored. Keep me in your prayers on this journey, as I pray for you with all my love. I'd like to thank my publisher and CEO of JNF Enterprises Leroy Mckenzie, Jr., for all the work put into making this book come to life. Words can't express my gratitude.

To my close friends who dared to believe in me. You kept me filled with your encouraging words, and I am blessed to have you in my life. I love you all dearly.

FORWARD

BACK FROM BROKEN

By no means am I perfect. I still
have flaws and areas that I am working
on. When I say back from broken I don't
mean this perfect person. What I mean is
who you are before you discover who you
are. That me I was when all the pieces had
to be put back together again.
Broken, hopeless, down and out, that feeling
you have of falling down and never being
able to get back up again.
That back from broken feeling is the best
because it's a feeling that no one can take
from you. It's the feeling of going through
So much and still be able to smile. You have
an understanding that there will be bad
days but it does not mean that you have a bad
life. When you can forgive and truly mean it
from your heart, you are, back from broken.
When you show love even when you
may not be loved, you are, back from broken.
When you can pick up the pieces and become
whole again, you are….

BACK FROM BROKEN

CHAPTER 1

LET THE CHURCH SAY..."A MAN"

It's 4:30am in the morning and I am wondering why it is so hard for me to begin to write this book? Why is that when I think of my life and the importance of releasing my thoughts into the atmosphere and how those who read this will be affected by what it is that I have to say, will they feel bitter towards me or will they act as if the stories never happened or did not take place? Even though no names are mentioned I know that those who are a part of the stories that I am telling will know who they are and the parts that they played in the situations that happened.

There came a point when I came to realize that I could not be worried about what others would think, I could not worry about the effect that it would have on their mental or psychological well- being but it was more important for me to focus on me becoming whole again and helping someone else become whole too. My wholeness and purpose outweighed their comfort. So many times we as people get so caught up in other people's feelings that we forget about our own feelings and we wind up crippling ourselves. We cripple ourselves mentally, emotionally, psychologically and spiritually.

The question that I began to ask myself now that I was in this conundrum is *HOW DO I GET UP FROM THIS MESS?"* My process to getting back to wholeness began with this premise and asking myself where will I be in 1 year if I took it one step at a time and began to work on me? I was bombarded with all these questions and I am going to take you on my journey and show you how I decided and got back from broken. When I decided to begin my journey I had to begin with where the battle originated from and that was in my mind. I had to start with a renewing of my mind and the way that I thought, spoke, acted and carried myself. The self-imprisonment that I had placed myself in had to be broken. You cannot begin to heal and get back from broken until you get to the core of where the brokenness began, most often that is in our minds.

I had let others control me in the past without a second thought or even acknowledging the fact that they were in control of me. There were so many years wasted because of this. I didn't know where to turn to or who to turn to which did not bold well for me because when one is in a state of brokenness we often cannot or do not think with a rational mind. We are distorted in many respects so therefore having someone to guide me out of the brokenness/darkness into the light/wholeness is what was missing.

No one seemed to recognize the hurt and pain that I was feeling on the inside because on the outside I was wearing the mask that covered it up and from the outside looking in everything seemed to be just fine. My parents, who of course loved and adored me, were not even able to recognize what I was going through on the inside of me. My church family didn't seem to take heed of what was going on with me either. The denomination that I was raised in

Holiness, was a denomination that felt as if they were always right. You dare not touch or approach the Pastor/Man of God, unless he wanted you in his circle. It was fire and brimstone if you watched a movie with your family and women were jezebels for wearing make-up or jewelry. There seemed to be something wrong with the way that the church was operating because while the congregation seemed to be poor or not doing so well, the preacher's pockets were getting fatter and fatter. This just didn't make sense to me.

I need for those of you who are reading this book to be real with me for a moment and understand what I am talking about. I am going to be 100% real with you in this book so I am warning you now if you are one of those people who thinks that the church or Pastors can do no wrong, you might want to close this book right now. In this book I am going to be as real and transparent as I can be and hopefully those of you who have chosen to keep on reading will understand where I was and where I needed to get to not just with myself but also with the church.

Most churches have secrets and the Holiness church is no different. Let me also say this, the Holiness denomination is the way to go as well. It is not perfect, just as any other denomination is not perfect and some of its ideals and way of thinking can be very archaic but it is also a denomination that focuses on keeping Christ first in your life and keeping him within your heart, mind and soul. While there were some preachers that had a fire and brimstone approach to the Holiness denomination, where there were a bunch of doe's and don'ts, they also neglected to also tell us about the God of Love and the God that is slow to anger not quick to use his wrath. It is very important that everyone know and understand who God is and not allow anyone or any religion to dictate to you the wrong answers about who God truly is.

Even with all of the things that may need to be worked on in our denomination at my church there was always the feeling of family. We had a closeness that was felt throughout the whole congregation. It was our own little secret society and no one else could come in. That closeness is what sometimes gets us through the rough and tough times that we may go through. I remember when I was a little girl; my parents and sisters were in a real serious accident. It left one of my sisters with many bones broken in her body; the other was knocked unconscious for some time and my mom's face was messed up almost to the point of non-recognition. My dad, who loves the Lord and serves him with all of his heart and soul, began to wonder how and why something like this could happen. It was a very trying time. When we went to pick my sister up from the hospital, after she had been there for a long time, he asked her where she wanted to go and she said that she wanted to go to church. My sister said that she wanted to go to church, so that is where we went. When we got to church and the pastor saw us coming in, they immediately made accommodations for my sister who was in the body cast.

The Pastor prayed for my sister and I know that she was not in that cast much longer after that. This is the closeness that our church had. Many of our church family would solicit their prayers and offer their words of encouragement to us. Our family went through some trying times and there were situations that came about that would test anyone's faith. My church had been there for us through this hard time and we were truly grateful for them being there in our time of need. But just as a church can be there for you they can also burden you too.

The church had made a decision that we were in need of a new facility because the old one that we were in was worn down and needed far to many improvements to keep on making repairs to it. The decision was made to build a 1 million dollar edifice and usher us into a new day in our church growth. Being that my dad was a master builder, he was tasked to oversee the work on the new church facility. My dad's faith in God and doing what he could for the church decided to leave his job and totally dedicate his time to the building of the new church. He is such a servant of God that serving God in this way was the only thing that he was going to do.

This was when I started to notice that the things that we had, we were slowly losing. We were a pretty well off family with my dad making good income but all that was going away with my dad leaving his job. My dad was not getting paid for the building of the church, which meant that income that he would have from working a regular job was not coming in and with my mom not working we had been totally dependent on my father's income. It became hard for us, but in spite of all of this my dad remained dedicated to the building of the church.

Things got so bad that we were without electricity for at least 9 months.

With all of this going on with my family the church did not even try to assist us with anything that we needed assistance with. There was not a word of encouragement or even a heartfelt prayer to help us with our situation. The only thing that seemed to be on the mind of the Pastor was getting that building built. Our church was the biggest church in the area and there were some other men in the congregation that gave of their time to assist in building the church but none seemed to be going through what we were going through. The church seemed to be taking many offerings during the many services that were held and I honestly believe that they had service on Friday's because it was payday. I know that you might be rolling your eyes at me right now but that is what I was thinking at that time.

At these services and even at the Saturday services there was an offering, tithes, building fund and pledges, missions, and pastor's appreciation offering. There were at least five to six offerings. Then after all of this took place the pastor would bring my dad to the front of the church and practically beg the congregation for $100 to pay him for the building of the church. I remember it was so frustrating and embarrassing not only for us but also for my dad as well.

It is one thing for a church to ask for multiple offerings but it was a whole new level when you bring someone before the church after all of this and ask them to give even more. The icing on the cake though was that the church would pretty much hold us hostage, which is what it felt like to me because we would be in church from 9am until 9pm in the evening sometimes and don't let the church not give the money that the pastor was asking to pay my father with and no one put in the money, no one would go anywhere until they collected that money.

The ironic thing about the collection of the money is, dad would give that little bit of money right back to the church for whatever they were asking for. There should never be a time that any church should conduct itself in such a way that people are shamed into giving when they had already given their all and there should never be a time where any individual or family should be embarrassed about their situation in front of the whole church. The church is not supposed to add to one's burden but it is supposed to lift them. Many churches seem to push the guilt trip on its congregants in order to raise the money it may need or even not need but to make a pastors life easier.

I know that I am talking a lot about my dad here to begin with but I can't help but think of all the sacrifices that this man made for his family and for the church and what he was burdened with. I can't even begin to understand what he was going through and what he endured. There was a resentment that began to build up on my part because there was a feeling of him not being there for me. I was a daddy's girl and my time with my dad was precious to me but when you are young you don't always understand what is going on.

There was definite demand on my father and it was in part from our pastor. He was a very charming pastor but also a very no nonsense pastor. What he said went and there were no questions asked. Those who may have even had the notion to question him were shunned or embarrassed. If he said that something wasn't to be done in the church than that thing was not to be done in the church or if there was something to be done in the church then it was done in the church. This was what I thought to be the modern day Pharisees way of living. These things tainted my way of looking at religion and my denomination. There seemed to be so many do's and don'ts that I almost felt like I did not like being Holiness. As I began to understand as I got older I realized that it was not the denomination that I was disliking it was those who were teaching and showing us who God was in this denomination. I love God with all of my heart and soul and it was not wrong for me to feel the way that I felt because of the misuse of the word of God to control others. This is no way for anyone to misuse God and manipulate others for your benefit.

I have always been a loner and everything that I have wanted to do and achieve was BIG!!! In reality I felt stuck and was hurting. Our church was hurting but our pastor was not hurting. There was a sense of needing to be free and that was the freedom that we as a church were seeking. We were stuck, we were crippled by religion.

CHAPTER 2
CRIPPLED BY RELIGION

Religion is such a litigious word. We put so much into what man says instead of what God says. Many think that having religion will get them into heaven, when this can be nothing further from the truth. We have to begin to understand the difference between religion and relationship. To many churches push religion and not relationship. We are being crippled by religion because many are believing what man is telling us instead of what God is showing us.

In this day and time many are looking towards what he, the Pastor, says instead of what God is saying to us. They take man's word as law versus what God's law truly says. We throw stones at each other, judge one another, down one another all in the name of religion. My question is, who is believing in Christ, who is believing in the Christ that died on the cross to save us from our sins? Christ's life was the light and has set the example that we all should live by. When we get caught up in religion we lose focus of that light and what we were born to do.

None of us are perfect; therefore, there is no perfect religion. There is something that we all should be doing. We should be setting the example for people instead of pointing the finger at each other or at those who are not in church. Our goal should be to be Holy, or different. We cannot expect anyone to be perfect, not our parents, not our friends and certainly not our Pastors. We are all fallible and susceptible to

19

sin. Our aim is to be like Christ and not judge others as Christ.

When you allow yourself to be crippled by religion you find yourself being ruled by all the do's and don'ts of religion. One will drive themselves crazy trying to keep up with everything that we should not do. This is why we cannot allow ourselves to get caught up in what many try and use to keep us bound within our service to God. When you lose sight of what we should be doing as what God's law says we should be doing you become someone that can be mis-educated about how you should carry yourself.

I must be honest and say that when I look back at my church that I attended in the past, there were hardly any movements that were made without consulting with the Pastor. It got to the point where they said that women should not wear T-shirts. This is real, and because the Pastor felt a certain way about his wife and didn't think that she should be able to wear t-shirts, it was pushed on the congregation in the same manner and there were other male members that tried to get their wives to adhere to the same type of thinking. There was even a time when he went to visit another church and all the women were wearing hats so he came back to our church and tried to make it so that all the women in the church were told to wear hats. Some went for it but others did not. This is the kind of miseducation that cripples individuals in religion.

People in that time didn't seem to have their own minds and allowed themselves to be told how they should see religion instead of gaining their own understanding of what a true Christian was and how they were to serve the Lord. Back then they fell for anything because they were crippled by religion and allowed themselves to be immobile in Christ word but directed by the Pastors words. We must not base our lives on the word religion and understand that we are all children of God. We should be following his beautiful example because when we do that we can no longer be entangled in the bondage of religion miseducation.

Getting caught up in the crippling of religion can cause one's bills to go unpaid just to support the Pastors lifestyle. When you are broken and seeking to find yourself you can allow people to make you feel as if who they are more important than who you are and your well-being. There should never go a time where you put anything or anyone before God or your well-being. This type of thinking is what many have done and some continue to do in this day and time in the church. This not only takes place in the church but in our society overall and brings people to the point where their mindset is not their owns but is that of someone else's. Getting back from this broken state of mind takes an understanding and a determination to come from under.

We must begin to get individuals to use their own minds and to think for themselves, read for themselves and use the 5 senses and the Holy Ghost guidance to understand what God's purpose is for us. If we do not do this and we allow ourselves to continue in this state of mind we will continue to be crippled by religion. How many people have not gone to the doctor because they were mis-educated about what they were told about the healing power of God so they did not get the proper care that they needed in order for them to get well.

There are those who think that seeking the doctors attention was not a way for God to get them better, when in fact had they gone to the doctor the very thing that they were seeking healing from could have been dealt with and they could have been cured from. Since they chose to not go see the doctor and to only believe that all they needed to do was pray and God would heal them they did not get the very healing that God had for them. This brokenness is what has kept many in the church Broken or even worse dying, either physically or just mentally.

Until people get tired of religion and the hypocrisy that is going on we will continue to be broken. So many continue to wear the mask and put on the façade so that no one really knows who they are and whose they are. How long will people in our congregations continue to keep lying to themselves? At some point you must tell the truth and know who you are. God already knows who we are at the core and we must understand that we cannot hide from him. We may be able to fool some but we cannot fool God and we must allow him to be our guide and not the religion that we profess to have.

Growing up in a church like that for me was detrimental to my well-being and how I perceived life to be. For me this began in my early childhood. What I was taught crippled me in my thinking and the way that I saw things. I remember our Sunday school teacher or Saturday school teacher, who was the Pastor's wife at the time saying to us that she had something that she needed to tell us. She began to tell us that her and the Pastor were going to be getting a divorce. We looked up to them as the standard of what a loving couple should be. I didn't know any other woman as my First Lady. This was not just me but the whole church had to accept this with no explanation as to why they were getting a divorce and what was going to happen from that point on.

This woman was the epitome of a God fearing woman to me. She was a woman who cared for the Homeless, who was a caretaker and all around great woman of God but no one dared ask the question why this was happening? The church wanted to give her a good bye party because of how special she was to us but the ministers of the church berated the church members who would attend the event. There were other things going on behind the scenes that some may or may have known about but many saw the after effect of the divorce. Despite the berating from the different Ministers of the church the members stood their ground and decided to show up for the special event that was being held for the out going First Lady. Not everyone went but there was a significant amount of people who came out in support of her.

I was so proud that we were allowed to attend and see how many people stood up for themselves by coming to the event and showing that they cared for our first lady. It can be difficult sometimes when you are in a state of brokenness to stand up for yourself but there will come a time in your life when you will "get sick and tired of being sick and tired," as my momma use to say. This memory has stayed with me since I was that young teenager who watched this happen in the church. Through that memory I learned that it is ok to ask questions, that it is ok to not go along just to get along. If you think that there is something wrong with what is going on, whether it be in your church, in your home, or on your job, ask questions and don't just accept anything that someone tells you.

We cannot just sit there and be a bump on the log and do nothing. When we do that we allow ourselves to be in the strangle hold that some people wish to keep us in. If we do nothing, then when something goes down you will be the one wondering what happened and why is this happening. It is happening because you chose to sit on the sidelines and accept being what others told you to be. All you have to do is open your eyes, open your ears and be aware of what is going on. The bible tells us to watch and pray not watch and *prey*. There is a difference and those who do not watch and pray can be preyed upon if they are not careful.

It's ok to not be an airhead and to think for yourself. It is ok to question authority and to question when we see something being done that is not right or in alignment with what the word says. There is a time and place for everything and you do have to be careful and mindful of how you approach a situation because there will certainly be those who will not like what it is that you may be saying or even why you are questioning their authority. Having a Pastor for a father has given me an understanding for a time and place for addressing things but it does not mean that they cannot be questioned or cannot be held accountable for their actions.

Pastors are God's men and women but it does not mean that they are necessarily called or walking in their anointing. Don't be confused by what some may say or what some may do who say that they are called by God. Some want the power, prestige, and presence that comes with the position of authority but some do not want the accountability that also comes with it and some will even abuse their power, prestige and authority to cripple people in their religion.

Back From Broken…   Rosheka Henry

CHAPTER 3
IDENTITY CRISIS
IN THE CHURCH

When I think of identity crisis in the church it breaks my heart. It breaks my heart because we don't really know who we are. How many people do you know in the church are going around and don't know what they are supposed to be doing in or for the kingdom? They don't have a clue where to begin. I know several, and I was one of them myself. Up until about a year and a half ago I didn't know or understand what God wanted me to do. When you don't know who you are in Christ you don't know how to defeat the devil. You don't really know the power that you have in Christ. There is this constant questioning and there is no sense of identity.

When you don't have your identity in Christ you are always susceptible to what the enemy will throw at you. You will always feel as if you don't know who you are or whose you are. This is why it is important that the church have a clear understanding of who it is and then ensure that its members know who they are. Let me give you a secular example of what I mean. When I was younger there was this basketball coach. He was well liked and he could pick and choose what he wanted to do at the time. With me being young and going through my identity crisis, this coach picked me. I didn't realize at the time that he had picked me. Things started to happen and I just felt like something wasn't right. Confused Christians sometimes blame themselves for things that may happen to them. We sometimes feel as if we had done something wrong to make God mad with us. We start to ask the question, did I do something to deserve what has happened to me? Our minds are made to feel as if we did something wrong and deserved what happened to us when that is the furthest thing from the truth.

I was fifteen years old and didn't know who I was in Christ. I just didn't believe that anyone would listen to me or believe me. This coach tried somethings with me and being the young student I was I didn't think that anyone would listen to me. No adult even noticed the look that I had been going around with on my face. When this coach tried these things I was able to curtail anything from happening but it still left me confused. I didn't know that I had a voice. I had been raised in a church where I didn't have a voice so why would things be different at school?

I kept this to myself. This scenario went on for three months. Not long after that one of my best friends one day while we were in class tapped me on the shoulder and asked me if I was alright. For whatever reason when she did this and asked me the question I began to break down and cry. From that moment on she became my voice. That night she went home and she told one of our favorite teachers that there was something wrong with me. When she told her this the next day this teacher and the coach were sitting there in the room. I didn't know that my best friend had told our teacher about me at the time but when she told her she evidently wanted to make sure that I was alright. When we were in the room she pulled her chair up next to me and asked me if I was ok. I told her that I was fine. After that she began to tell me a story about her past and this authority figure who did something to her. I didn't understand why she was telling me this story but it worked because I broke down and told her everything that had gone on.

As a result of this the coach was fired and do you know that there were students and even teachers that were upset with me because of what had happened. Students didn't want to talk to me and teachers even began to treat me so coldly after that. My dad didn't want me to have to endure this kind of treatment because of the way that I was made to feel. There was one of my teacher's sons who was on the football team that I was friends with who saw the way that I was being treated and would walk with me to my classes to ensure that people did not mess with me or start anything with me.

My advice to anyone out here who may have gone through or is going through something similar to this is to be careful. There are predators out here that will seek to kill and destroy you. I thank God that this man was not able to penetrate me and do whatever else that he may have wanted to do to me. God was watching out for me in this situation but not everyone has had the same result as I did. This same man some years later connected with me on social media and asked for my forgiveness. I had forgiven him before this because that was who I was in Christ.

Don't be confused about anything in the body of Christ. We have a voice and we must know and understand that your voice will be heard by your father and that your voice in the world can be heard as well. Never feel as if you have done anything wrong in these situations. Women I want you to hear me, say something, young girls, say something and those of you who are in the church say something!!! Do not think that just because you are young or just because it maybe someone in authority who says something wrong or does something wrong that they are not to be held accountable. When the church knows who it is in Christ you will have those who may not know or understand themselves completely to begin to identify themselves and know who they are.

CHAPTER 4
THE PRODICAL DAUGHTER

In this chapter I will be very transparent with you. There will be things that I will share with you that hopefully will help you and will give you some insight as to the things that went on with me and some choices that I made that were wrong and some choices that were not the best choices for me to make at that time. I knew what I was up against when I was going through what I was going through but in spite of I kept on.

With the decisions that I made I found those in the church to be judgmental and cast this dark cloud over me. Now, as I tell you these things I hope that I am able to help someone, free someone and empower someone. Hopefully by me telling you my story in this book you will be equipped with the knowledge and tools that you will need to either get out of a similar situation or situations or not get into any of these situations. My intent is for you to come away from reading this better than you were before you read this book.

As I talked about it in the last chapter, the situation with this school coach, this was my first sexual encounter and as you can imagine, this can be very traumatic for a young girl. When a young girl's first encounter with sex is one of this nature it has a lasting effect on her life. Some may recover from it and others may be so traumatized by it that they never recover from it. No matter the individual girl or woman for that fact, they are never the same.

With my situation it completely blew my mind. I never went to therapy, which can really be a benefit for anyone who has encountered this kind of situation. There is this stigma that is associated with therapy and mentally dealing with this kind of traumatic situation. This is not something that should be taken lightly nor should it be swept under the rug. Please hear me when I say this. For any woman who has or is going through this kind of situation, get help. There is nothing wrong with seeing and talking with someone about what has happened to you and to have them assist you in getting through it.

To many of us think that we can handle it but in reality we never deal with it and let it fester for years and years and years and it just builds up inside of us until the body can no longer hold it and it must let it go in some way shape or form. If you are someone who has a child that has experienced this or is experiencing this type of situation, get them some counseling. No matter what they tell you get them some counseling. Do not allow them to bottle all of that toxic energy inside of them. They may not thank you now but trust me they will thank you later.

It is very important that you do something to help yourself in these situations. If you do not get the help that you need you will spend the rest of your life thinking that it was your fault. You will continue to ask the question, what did I do wrong? You have to be bold enough and brave enough to get the help you need so that you can begin to be whole again. The best way to ensure that you can move past the pain, bitterness, resentment and anger is by having someone help you to deal with it.

I found myself leaving the school that I was attending and the school that this coach had been fired from. Unfortunately the school that I would attend was a school in the same town as this coach lived. Now, this is a very small town so everyone knew who I was even before I got to this school, because of the popularity of the coach and what had happened. As you can imagine I wasn't there very long and I was not able to graduate from high school but I was able to get my GED.

Once I received my GED I entered college and I was on my own and had my first taste of freedom. Not knowing and experiencing many things for the first time I began to want to do and be a part of things. When I returned home during breaks and other times I felt that weight that had been on me before all over again. It was hard to escape the past and I allowed it to imprison me. Just when it seemed that those things were behind me things show back up again.

I am back at school again and my roommate comes into the room and tells me that there is a man in a suite downstairs for me. As I scurried to try and find a skirt to put on, because I thought it was my dad and I didn't want him to know that I had begun to wear pants, I quickly found one and got down stairs to meet this gentleman. To my surprise it was a friend of my dad's. My first thought was that something is wrong or something happened. Well, he asked me to come outside to his car, so I followed him out to his car and got in. My first question was, what's wrong?

He said to me, "nothings wrong, it's nothing like that." He then starts to say, I know that you are a college student and that you could use some extra money, and he proceeds to pull out a thousand dollars. He then says to me, "if you will go to a hotel with me and have sex with me I will give you this thousand dollars." What would you do? He was right I needed money and I did need it bad. This would help me to be able to do some of the things that I wanted to do at school.

I had to ask myself, what was going on? How bold was this man to come and see me at school and ask me to have sex with him. This is someone who was a church member and had been to my parent's house and that I served food and drink to. Where did this come from, who does this? I truly didn't understand it. I had never felt comfortable around him before and now I truly understand why. So, what did I do? I went back up to my dorm room and talked to another friend of mine who was in her room and to get her opinion on what I should do. She told me that she got these offers all the time and it was how her and some others got money and that I was stupid for not taking the offer.

Well feeling the pressure and needing the money I called the man back and accepted his offer. As we got into the situation I changed my mind. I told him that this was all wrong and that I didn't want to do it. Can you imagine what he was thinking? What may have been going through his mind? Here he is a friend of my parents, a member of our church and all of a sudden I say no. He was surely thinking that I would go and tell someone about this whole situation and that I may even try and say that he did something that he didn't do. So, as you can imagine, he got upset and he did proceed to try and rape me. We, as women, have to be careful of the situations that we do put ourselves in. I am by no means trying to justify what he did and what he tried to do but I put myself in a dangerous situation.

I fought him and fought him for what seemed like forever and he eventually stopped and something came over him and he said to me, "I can't do this, I can't face your daddy." As a reflect on this situation I know that I should not have listened to that young lady that had given me the bad advice. Eventually he took me back to the campus and basically kicked me out of his car, I went into the dorm, took a shower and cried and began to get angry with the world. The sad but crazy thing about this whole story is that this same man not long after our encounter was locked up for raping another young lady. Can you imagine my thoughts when I found this out? I was thrown aback by it. Please, if you find yourself in this kind of situation get help but even before you get in the situation realize that you do not have to sell yourself in order to get the things that you need.

Moving on from this situation, I began to try and find myself. I had a boyfriend now and I was searching. I was praying and talking to God and began to try and seek his guidance in what he wanted for me. I want everyone that is reading this to understand that when you seem to be out in the darkness that you must trust God to bring you back to where he wants you to be. There will be situations and circumstances that you can't change and you must move past them.

So, I am back on campus one afternoon and there is a group of us that would hang out or study together in this particular area on campus. There was racial tension on this campus and it was very racially divided so most of the blacks hung with blacks and whites hung with whites. This particular afternoon I was sitting outside in this area and across from me is this white guy, who is pretty well known on campus and someone that was known by my boyfriend at the time. My boyfriend and I would meet at this area after class and wait for the others to join us or we would just hang out and chill on our own. On this particular day the guy that was sitting across from me strikes up a conversation with me and we have a good interesting conversation together.

After our conversation he goes on into the dorm and is gone so I really didn't think anything of it because my boyfriend would be coming soon. After a while my boyfriend still hadn't shown up so I didn't know what had happened to him, I was thinking maybe he got tied up somewhere with a class or something. So, after a long while the white guy comes back out and tells me that my friend is waiting for me up in his room. As we are headed towards the dorm he tells me that he had something that he wanted to give to me. Me being young and naive I say ok, and proceed to follow him, not paying attention that we were not headed towards my friends dorm room. We get to the white guy's dorm room and he says he has something for me in his room. I again say, ok, step inside and next thing that happens he has me on his bed and begins to try to rape me.

As I am kicking and screaming at him to get off of me and saying, "why are you doing this to me", he tells me that he has always wanted a black girl and that I was the one. He said that he had been watching me and that I was the one. As we are struggling again God intervened and he stops and gets up and then tells me to get the hell out of his room. After this ordeal I ran to my room and I couldn't even cry anymore. I just began to get angry and more angry. I never told anyone about this and held all of this bitterness inside of me.

By this time I began to take on the mindset that people will always just try and take what they want from you. I just began to get tired. I was tired with my life, I was tired of the church, I was tired of home. I was just through with everything. My life was in total darkness. I couldn't see anyway yet alone the way. I couldn't fight anymore. I kept telling my friend that I was tired. He kept asking me what was wrong but I would never talk to him about it. This showed me that no one can or will get help until they are ready to. They have to make up in their mind that they need to get help or that they want to get help. My friend tried to be a source of help for me but I just wasn't ready.

As you can imagine after all of this I was all confused. I was confused about the church and what it was supposed to be doing. I started to resent it. I resented the restrictions and all the other things that I thought religion did to you. I wanted to be as far away from the church as possible. I was so resentful of the church and everything that was back home. My mom was scheduled to come and pick me up from campus but my desire was not to go home. I just didn't want to go home. My friend came by my dorm room and I told him that I was tired and that I didn't want to go home. He said that he would buy me a bus ticket and that I could come home with him. I made a decision that I would go with him. I knew that my mom was coming to get me but my desire was not to go home. I knew that my mom was going to freak out if I wasn't there when she got to the campus. So, we headed out and sho nuff mom got to the campus and was looking for me. She had the whole campus looking for me and when she finally couldn't find me she left.

I just wanted freedom and I felt that I would not get it if I went back home. My intension was to never go home again when I left, but God had other plans for me. I had been gone for about a month or so and I had not called or talked with my parents. I had pretty much run away from home. I was introduced to this guy that was a friend of my friend. As we were there at the house the guy came into the kitchen and asked me did my parents know that I was there? I said no. they told me that I needed to call home. Well, that was all I needed to hear because I started to head straight for the door. They finally convinced me to call home but I didn't call my parents. I called my grandma but not my parents. I talked with her and she told me that I needed to call home. I didn't call them but they called me and I spoke with them. Soon after that I was on the bus on my way back home.

That bus ride gave me a long time to think and to contemplate what might happen once I got back home. Once I arrived we headed home and the ride there was very quiet. When we arrived home, nothing was said that night and I tried to get my dad to let out any anger that he was feeling for me out that night, so I set my bags right at the front door. My dad didn't say a word. My mother was the one that let into me and gave me a piece of her mind. Sometimes when we are in our darkness we hurt those around us, whether intentionally or unintentionally. I didn't have the right mindset at this time so I didn't care about how anyone else was feeling but me. I didn't care about the ramifications all I cared about was how I was feeling.

Once back home I eventually started to go back to my church again. There was a different feeling at this time though. The church was going through some issues itself and I didn't want to deal with that but I did still stay. In my decision to stay I was introduced to a guy who was going to be the brother in law of my pastor. We hit it off and I fell for him because I thought that he could be my way out. After just a month of dating we got married.

After some time we decided we were going to head to Texas. We picked up our things and we were going to the Lone Star State. I was pregnant at the time too and all I can remember is that I was free. We were there for a while but then we were headed back home to Alabama. When you are young you make decisions without any thought of the consequences that come with it. I was searching for something and the more I searched for it the further it seemed to be from me.

My husband and I went out to California for a visit and I totally loved it. I wanted to be in

California, but while we were out there, there all of a sudden was this really bad feeling that I was getting. God was showing me in his way that I needed to get out. Needless to say my husband and my father in law didn't like or want to hear that. Eventually we got on a bus and were headed back to Alabama. Shortly after that my husband and I would no longer be together.

When I tell you that I was broken, I was broken at this point. I was pregnant with my daughter and about to have her, my husband and I were separated on our way to a divorce and he informs me that he is moving back out west. The only thing that got me through this broken time in my life was God. We have to understand that when everyone else seems to have left you God is still there with you. He has promised us that he would never leave us nor forsake us. Whenever we need him he is always right there for us, we just have to know to call on him.

I was getting it all together again. I was back in school again and getting straight A's. I was now in Atlanta and was getting many opportunities but I was turning them down. My mindset was that it wasn't what God wanted for me. I was making a living for me and my little girl but I was still working through getting back from broken. I encourage you to pray about the decisions that you make and don't think that God is saying no to everything. There will be times that you will have to step out on faith and believe in where God is leading you. Understand that God is going to lead you where he wants you to be.

Sometimes we can allow our beliefs to cripple us and keep us from moving forward in our life. You can't allow others to influence you to the point where you can't even make a decision. Understanding who you are is critical in being able to make sound decisions. Our experiences can influence us and the way we make decisions. There were incidents that did influence my decisions. I can't even begin to explain how important it is for me to see the decisions I was making and why I was making them. Part of my hang up in my decision making was my issue with authority figures. Up into recently I still had my issues with those in authority. These issues come from my dealings with those in authority in the church and the things that happened and people either seeing or not seeing and saying nothing.

It is very crucial that those who are in authority understand the power and influence that they have over others. Some will take that power and influence and try to abuse it. I have had some very close people who were in authority take that power that they had and try to abuse it with me. They felt as if they could over step their boundaries and cross that threshold and become more than what they should have been trying to be with me. There were other authority figures in the church that I had been disappointed by and that is what had been filling my heart with bitterness. I felt betrayed and bitter because these people who I looked up to were not there for me, I did not feel protected.

This is how God works things out and will keep watch over you. There were issues with the church that I was attending and those issues came about because of the way in which I believe that they were doing things in the church. When we are out of

41

order God has a way of showing us and if we do not heed his calling then we will not be successful. Nothing that you do will work out if you are not in order with what God says. The decisions that I would be making were all influenced because of the order that I was trying to be in.

After being in Atlanta for some time my dad thought that it would be better to move back to Alabama. We made that move and I began again to build a life again for me and my daughter. I had gotten a job working at the local hospital and getting my life back on track. I then met a man that would take me through the next four years of mental anguish. This was an older man so there again was this authority figure that I was so against. I didn't recognize it at that time but the choice in being with this man had to do with that very thing. We got into a relationship and he treated me like a Queen in the beginning but all that changed after a while. He was in the military and served our country. He became very controlling and mentally abusive and would do things that I would not wish on my worst enemy. This man became so jealous and did not want anyone to even look at me. There were times that he would threaten me by putting a gun to my head, taking me to a lake and telling me that he was going to blow my brains out and no one would even find me.

This man was so abusive that he would even put a knife to my throat and threaten to kill me. In spite of the way that this man treated me I still decided to marry him. Can I tell you how broken that I was. My self-esteem was so low that I allowed this man to physically abuse me and one time came to the point where I found myself in the bathtub and this man urinating on me and I did nothing. While this man was married to me he would see other women. There was one time that he even picked me up and threw me out of the house onto the concrete, where I sprained my tailbone after I caught him with another woman. He had me to the point where I still remained with him and was afraid to get out.

Now that have had years to think about this situation it is one that I think that was not only abuse on his part but it was also a mental health issue too. There are some military veterans that come back from war or wars and have difficulty dealing with civilian life and don't get the help that they need. I believe that my husband at the time was one of those men who needed help but unfortunately did not get the help he needed and as a result his issues were taken out on me. This is a very dangerous situation to be in if you are a spouse to someone like this and you must get out!!! You cannot save them and you cannot help them. They need to seek professional help and you put your life and your children's lives in danger if you stay.

I tell you these things not to give you a graphic description but to tell you the truth about situations and hopefully you can avoid them or get out of them. Despite everything that I was going through I continued to play the fool and wear the mask. I put on the smile and acted as if everything was perfect. There were a few people that knew something was going on but they didn't know exactly what but every- one else had no idea what I was going through. In every abusive relationship there sometimes comes a tipping point and I knew that this tipping point would come for me. I had been taking it and taking it and on this particular day he was on one of his rants. We were arguing to the point that I just got up and walked out of the bedroom and went into the kitchen. My husband followed behind me and so I grabbed the sharpest knife that I could find to stab and kill this man. When I turned around to head back into the bedroom, I noticed that he was right there in the kitchen with me. He froze and didn't make a move. He asked me to just put the knife down. As we both stood there I began to think about what would happen to my kids if I did this to this man?

As I began to think more and more about my kids and the consequences that would come if I did kill this man, I froze and couldn't move. I eventually put the knife down and then we went back to the same ole same ole again. Well, maybe a day or so later he was back at it again and we proceeded to argue. This man was so mean and twisted that he would take out all of his anger and frustration on me. We people have to understand that hurt people will hurt anyone that is around them regardless of who it is. I was that person for this man, my husband. While materially I had everything that I wanted or needed but emotionally, physically and psychologically I was at the bottom.

We were arguing at this particular time and this man so tormented me that he told me that he had given me aids and it stopped me dead in my tracks. I was taken aback by this and he knew that this would do this to me and that is exactly what he wanted to do. So after a little while he pulls out his military medical records and shows me that he is in perfect health and that he did not have aids. He would do things like this to try and torture me and mentally abuse me. Within that same week I would go to the doctor and get a physical for myself to ensure that I did not really have aids and thank God that those records did come back ok and everything turned out fine.

There are many who will say, see I told you so about all that has happened to me. There are some that will say that I got what I deserved but you have to understand the root of the decision making. My decisions were made from a place of hurt. That hurt that began when I was much younger. We have to understand that if we do not deal with our hurts at the roots, than we will continue to make decisions out of that same hurt. As a consequence we will continue to dig a deeper and deeper hole that we just can't get from out of. When you deal with the hurt at its root; then you will find yourself released from all of your hurts and headed back from broken.

Well, how did I get myself out from under this man that had this uncontrollable power over me? I first found my breakthrough at my dad's church on a Wednesday evening. He had been praying for my well-being and God's spirit seemed to hit me in that service and I felt hope again. I woke up the next morning and began to read the bible. As I began to read the bible, Isaiah Chapter 54, I began to cry like a baby. God finally touched me somewhere in my heart and allowed me to let the pain I was feeling out through my tears. I felt the yoke of the bondage that I was in begin to be released. I prayed to God and told him that if he created the way out that I was going to leave and not look back. Not even a week later I found myself packing a few things up for me and the girls and just left. This man would come home to a house full of furniture and all the material things that were there but empty of me and my girls. I took my girls and a few things and I never looked back. It was not easy and has not been easy but I knew that the best thing for me and those girls was to get us out of that toxic situation. I do not believe that I would have lived had I not left this man.

The thing with all of this to was that my mind was so messed up that there was even a time where I had tried to commit suicide and not only was I going to take my life I was going to take my girls along with me. Even though I may have had those intensions, God had other plans for me. The attempt was not successful as you can tell as you are reading from this book right now about me but it had taken me over four years to get over what this man had done to me. I had gotten to the point where I hated men and didn't want to have anything to do with a man. My mom told me that I really needed time to myself and to just focus on me and the girls.

Well, some years had gone by and this same man that put me through all that he put me through contacted me and he actually has given his life to Christ and is a preacher now. He apologized for the things that had happened and told me that God had whipped him for touching his anointed child, which was me. He also offered to pay for anything that was needed by the dance group that I had begun. He let me know that he was a dark and sick man back then and that he was thankful for me praying for him. I had been praying for him all along and I am grateful that God did save him. I learned to let it go as many of you need to do in order to get back from broken. The only way to get back from broken is to let it go. Had I still been holding onto the bitterness and anger that had built up I would not have been able to move on and get out of that black hole of bitterness. Getting closure to this part of my life was what God felt I needed and that is what he gave me.

The Lord had moved so much in my life that I had begun to put the pieces back together. I happen to be at the grocery store and I saw the President of the hospital that I had worked for. We checked out and he headed to his car and I headed towards mine. I stopped and started heading towards the president. I stopped him and explained my situation to him about making a bad decision and how I left the hospital and I was looking to get back into the hospital. He pulls out a piece of paper and tells me to call the office on Monday and shortly after that I received a phone call from the hospital to come into the hospital for an interview. I go in and needless to say I received the job and I was on my way back.

As I am working at the hospital, I met a man one day that I thought was everything that I wanted in a man. He was taking care of his mother and we began a conversation and started to get to know one another. You gotta follow me hear ladies because I am going somewhere. Well, as time went on we got closer and closer I began to fall for this man, this married man!!! How and why did I have to spend the last four years working on me and getting my life together just to fall in love with this married man. Why did I find myself having feelings for this guy who was spoken for and why couldn't I let the feelings go and just leave it alone.

If I had just taken a little longer getting to work that morning that we met or had made a stop along the way maybe there would not have been an encounter. That encounter had to happen though. If that encounter had not happened, than I would not have my son right now, who is one of the joys of my life. No, the situation or circumstance by which he is here is not something that I am happy about but there is nothing that brings me more joy than to see my son and his handsome smiling face.

So as you can see the relationship that resulted in my son was not one that I am proud of. Can you imagine the church world and the things that may have been said or were said? Even though those who maybe reading this or even those who are in the church may look down on me for the decisions that I made but I serve a God that is forgiving. I want you to realize that the God we serve loves us and will forgive us if we ask. All we have to do is ask. I know he forgave me as soon as I asked. God showed me and told me that he would be with me every step of the way. He said yes, there are consequences to the choices that you made but I will be there with you.

Even though my son is four going on five years old and it has been that long since I have been in this situation, there are still people who have their mouth on the situation. There are many people that will continue to talk about you even after God has delivered you from them. Hear me when I say this, don't let people control the way you feel about your past. When God says that he is done with it, it is over with. There is no one else that needs to have a say in the matter. You don't have to answer to anybody else other than God about your past. If he has forgotten it than you should too!!

We serve an unconditional loving God and even though people love us conditionally he says that we are his. Despite the mistakes, despite the wrong choices, he still loves me and he still loves you. There was a reason that I had to go through everything that I am telling you right now. Had I not gone through what I talked about in this chapter and the other chapters as well, you would not be reading this book right now. This book was not for me but it was for those of you who maybe going through any of the situations that I talk about here and it helps you get out of it or not get into it. I want you to be better and not have to go through the same hurt, anger and bitterness that I went through. Through all the frustrations and all the hurt I still smile, and I am still standing.

Well, one day my sister came to me and asked me to do some praise dancing. I wasn't even thinking about praise dancing and knew nothing about it. This was for our pastor's, dad's anniversary. I looked into what this praise dancing was and my sister sent me this song, "Take Me To The King" and as I began to listen to the song and think of dancing to it, I began to fall in love with Praise dancing and this is how I came to start the dance group "Warriors of Praise."

CHAPTER 5
WARRIORS OF PRAISE...DANCING A NEW DANCE

I walked through the home office, my sister sitting at the computer called me by my nickname, which is Shan. She began to talk about my dad's Pastors Anniversary that was approaching. She had thought of a different idea. She had thought of doing something we had never done before in our church. Jennifer wanted us to do a praise dance to Tamela Mann's song, "Take Me To the King." "Wow, that sounds great, I said. When are you going to get started on it?" "She replied back with an answer that I had never expected. She said, well Shan I was kind of hoping you would head this up for us." After looking at her for a few seconds like she had lost her mind, I respectfully declined the request. OK, maybe not so respectfully. It was more like a loud "NALL! Girl, I can't praise dance. When have you ever seen me praise dancing and now you want me to lead a group of people. You do it!" She told me to think about it. I told her I didn't need to at all.

A few hours went by, and for some reason her request continued to come before me. I kept dismissing it of course, like we so often do when God is trying to push us into our destiny. I can say that I tried to fight it for a while before I finally went back to her and told her I'd give it a try. I was still very doubtful that this would ever work. Especially with me being so hard on myself all the time. I just felt like if I did it, then it may come up short. Nevertheless; I decided to step out there on faith. May I tell you, that I had no idea that I just accepted part of my destiny. Right there, at that very moment, without having a clue as to what I was doing, God opened the door to a whole new chapter in my life. Although I didn't want to accept the challenge before me, God had enough mercy on me, to tug at my heart. He could've just as easy let Jennifer give up on the idea.

He knew that this was a path that I had to take. God knew that this would be my defining moment. My turn around, my start to healing. I praise Him so much for that! How many times do we give up on the first, second, or third "no?" To say the least, the praise dance turned out absolutely beautiful with me and thirteen young ladies and kids. At this point, we still had no name. We just danced.

As time passed on different young women started to ask about how they could be a part of this group. I honestly thought it was fascinating, yet I felt nervous. It just felt like I had no control over the growth of the group. God did. So, I had a few girls that were not a part of the church at that time to join, and I was more than happy to have them. I just felt like the group was helping young people that needed a positive way to release some of the stress of everyday life. Maybe God could use me to be a blessing in any form or fashion He chose. I was a willing vessel. People started to call upon the group to travel different places, and that humbled me. God was doing this, not me. I particularly remember being at one of the church's we had to dance at, and while a few of the girls and I were taking pictures, one of the dancers asked me, "What's the name of our group Shan?" I looked at

Tomeka and said, I don't even know, I've been thinking of a few names, but they don't seem to fit. All of a sudden, I just felt overwhelmed to ask Tomeka to think of a name for our group. People that know me know that usually I'm very picky about who does what in our dance group. They call me a perfectionist at dance rehearsals, but in my heart, I just want us to be as close to perfect as we possibly can because we are dancing before The King of Kings and heaven.

I was a bit surprised that I asked her, but I know for a fact, that it was God's doing. She went outside for some reason, and when she came back inside the church, she said, " I thought of a name for our group, what about Warriors of Praise?" If she could remember the way I looked at her when I said, "That's it! That's our name, Warriors of Praise." I was talking to her outwardly, but what she didn't know was that inwardly, I was telling God, that's it. He had been tugging on my heart about not just picking some random name, but He was going to choose our name. He let me know that He had ordained this group. He used Tomeka to name our praise dance group. When the name left her lips, my heart jumped because I heard what God was telling me, and I am so glad that He allowed me to hear His voice and I'm especially glad that she was in a place to allow God to use her to name Warriors of Praise.

You may be wondering why I spent a little time on how our group got its name. I am about to tell you. Let me say this, when God ordains you for a task, the devil gets upset to see that task going forth victoriously. When I tell you this praise dance group was on another level, I am not telling you just some story that sounds good to the ear. I'm telling you that people were being blessed through our dancing. I'm telling you that we've seen grown hard men crying after we danced, and standing outside the aisles, just waiting to give one of us a hug because their lives were touched. People felt God in the building when Warriors of Praise dance, and trust me; these girls were being drilled on giving God His glory back. Our pastor had private meetings with the praise dancers. Teaching us why we are dancing, how to dance effectively, how to invite the Holy Ghost in before he even takes the pulpit. How we can tear down hard walls with what we were doing. We were fasting and praying together. We were one. We were sisters. Even our little girls group was anointed to dance. We had been on television stations, being interviewed about praise dancing.

How many times have you seen praise dancers being interviewed on major networks as well as local viewed by hundreds and thousands of people? Yes, it happens, but it's so rare. Do not think I'm lifting up flesh here, because you are about to see why I'm going in this direction. All this glory I'm talking about here, Jesus has already received it back ten times over. This is my testimony. I remember getting up between the hours of 3a.m. and 5a.m. almost every morning. Praying that God would continue to keep His arms around us, and His favor over our group. I knew the enemy was lurking. I knew he was upset. That is why I sacrificed all that I knew how, just praying that we could survive the attack that would come our way.

God woke me up one morning, and I heard Him speaking just as clear as I've heard Him several times before. He gave me a message to tell the ladies that danced, starting with me. He said to me, "I have granted the angels to dance with each one of you. Only know that my eyes are watching each and every one of you closely. Do not shame my name." It was something about the way God said the word, "closely" that rattled me to the core. I felt as if I was this tiny person that had this gigantic person holding a microscope over me, watching whatever I did, and whatever I said.

My challenge was to tell the dancers what the message was for our group. Oh sure, God granting His angels to dance with us was phenomenal within itself. But how do you make it stick in their ears that because He's granting us such favor, He's also keeping an eye on us? How do you make people feel the urgency or importance the way you felt when it was given to you? Sometimes I feel as though I failed that task. Maybe I didn't stress it enough. I will say this. God kept His word to us. We would dance and reports would come back from people that witnessed us dancing. They would say that they saw us dancing, but they didn't see anybody's feet! Some would say they saw angels dancing beside us. I'm not lying! This happened for real. I have to many witnesses. God being the main one. Different girls in my group would be struggling with a part at rehearsal, and be so nervous whenever we went to pray before we danced. We would say, remember the angels are dancing with us. There is video evidence all over the internet where these same girls would do their part, and we go back and look at the videos in awe, just for the girls to confess, that wasn't me doing that. I have no idea how I did that. I felt something or someone beside me doing that. But it wasn't me, it was God helping me.

God was doing it, and people were getting help. We were in such demand to dance at everyone's program until my pastor pulled me aside several times and said, "pray about the places you go, people are doing this for competition, and we will not dance for a show." I heard him, but I didn't hear him clearly. All I saw was God moving and helping people and the dancers in their own lives. I wanted to keep that flow steady. I failed to listen to wisdom, I must say. Our schedules stayed full, our rehearsals would last sometimes three and four hours. We would sometimes have practice three and four times a week it depended on how big the event was we had to minister at. God continued to bless me with creative ways to choreograph dances that had a message. We just didn't dance to any song, we danced to whatever God put in my spirit and gave me the choreographing for. He would show me moves that came to life over time. My dancers would think I had gone completely crazy with some of these ideas, and all I would tell them to do was trust me.

These ladies did just that. They trusted me, even when they didn't know why. Once these dances were completed you'd see it come to life, and everyone witnessed God's power through a dance. I didn't choreograph every single dance or come up with every single move, but what God gave us, He gave it to us in a mighty way. He completely gets the glory, honor, and praise for all He's done for us.

Now that I have told you about this group that seemed so unbreakable. Let me begin my reason for telling you. The power of God can be evident in your life, as it was this praise dance group. But it's up to you to keep it that way. You must do your part. If you do not, you will witness the rise and fall of something so divine in your life, and if you do, trust me, it will shake you to the very core. Listen to God. Know His voice, follow Him at all times. Trust Him even when it is not the popular thing to do. All the stories I have told you about "Warriors of Praise" don't you know Satan was mad? Don't you know that attacks were all around us? The troubles that hid within our group surfaced over and over again. Yet, God would still be consistent in moving for us. Inside, my heart was tearing apart. I felt that I was all alone. I was driving forty five minutes each way to practices, plus church and any other event we had, over and over again. I was dragging three children around with me. Sometimes, they would get right off the bus from school, just to get in the car and go. They were tired and I was tired. But I just felt like I had to keep going because it was what God wanted for me.

I was becoming bitter because I felt like my hard work wasn't getting noticed at all. The group was discouraged and at odds with each other, everything was falling apart before our very eyes. It was one of the most miserable times I remember going through. To feel unappreciated, but work all the harder to prove that I am not a quitter either. I see the group is in all different directions and falling away one by one, but pride tells you, ok, we'll just keep going on strong, all while you are torn up inside. It's hurtful to see people that once stood behind you become your enemy. You wonder what you've done, or didn't do. People that you feel should've had your back, because they know your heart, leave you to fight this battle on your very own. What do you do when nobody but a mere handful is encouraging you to keep fighting, and don't become bitter in this process? What do you do when you keep repeating the voice of God's instructions in your head and hearing Him say my eyes are on each one of them? Yet, you see as a whole, the group somehow failed. Guess what? I'm the leader so guess who's to blame, regardless of efforts.

My days grew colder, resentful, and darker. God, why did you let this happen? You saw my heart from the beginning. You saw all I wanted was to please you. I wanted to help others. I wanted to help young women on the street find refuge in you, through my dancing. You let everyone that I thought was for me turn their backs, with the exception of a handful. I'm hearing who said what about me and I'm broken to pieces.

I…. I…. I… How horrible I felt. Yet trying to stand strong, while keeping every single ounce of bitterness that consumed me, within. My passion was being sucked dry and I didn't have the strength to fight for it any longer. So, an opportunity presented itself. A chance to bring hope back to a group that suffered a blow. I didn't want any of the girls to miss out so I called a meeting for them to come back. Let's see where this takes us. Maybe we can finally help lots of people like we all wanted from the beginning. The opportunity was promising, and it felt like an answered prayer. Finally, God had sent me some help. The weight I carried was just to much for me at that time. I'd never gone up against anything like that before in my life. So, I heard the proposition set before me, I let them hear it, everyone agreed by mouth that we should try and we did. Sure, I prayed as instructed before making any decision. They say they prayed with me as well and felt a peace too. Maybe they were being led by my feelings toward things. I'll take responsibility for that.

Now, here we are; a group again. I couldn't be more happier. Thank you Lord for bringing us together again. Each lady had her own special place and personality that only she could bring. It made us who we were. Now if we could just stay together, adding new people would be a blessing. One of our dreams was to start a dancing ministry for girls on the street that needed somewhere to turn. What we thought would be the beginning of a renewed dance group turned out to be the ending for a long time. We danced to Tamela Mann, "I Can Only Imagine," which was our most highly requested song! Our Pastor still loves it to this very day. God gave me every single move, and it has had its share of touching hearts. This time was different though. We looked at the video, and I noticed on the pulpit which we danced on, there were lights shining down on us. Yes, the pulpit itself had lights on it, but this was way to perfect, the way they shined on each one of us to be pushed aside as pure coincidence. On the trip home I showed the video to everyone, and no, my eyes were not playing tricks on me. Everyone saw those bright lights. It appeared to come straight from heaven. We danced with all our hearts that day, and then it was the end.

After I had swallowed the last dose of hurt, I left my daddy's church. Every piece of what I called my heart was shattered, shocked, and down-right confused. It just was no more left to give. I'd given all I had at that time. It didn't get me anywhere but frowned upon and I was still trying to figure out the why? I didn't care at all anymore; at least that's what I said on the outside. But on the inside, I just wanted to start over with me and my children. I was trying to hold on to something that really didn't want me and I felt like it was starring me right in the face. Oh, the road wasn't easy, but it was ok, it was no worse than my past position. So I found refuge in an unlikely source. I decided to take the opportunity presented for us, alone. What choice did I have now? They were a blessing to my family and me. I truly saw many venues to dance on. People were still getting help, and my little family seemed to be getting along okay. They miss home and so did I, but it was for the better of the church that I left, right? People were happy we left my own daddy's church anyway. Correct? You do see where I'm going with all of this don't you? If not, then hang on tight.

Oh life was passing me by. I was meeting new people, and new people were loving my children and me. I was ministering dance on stages I never would have thought could be possible. People from all over the country were wanting my new group, Once again, t.v. interviews were being presented to me and that was ok with me. Yet, something was missing. I was mentoring an up and coming artist and she needed what I had to give. She ran after the knowledge, and I felt appreciated. I hadn't felt this in a while, so I was totally accepting of all the love the church gave us. They were a genuine people, and I met lifetime friends there. I obtained my teaching certification and was gearing my mind towards obtaining a degree in Theology. I was speaking before people, and I was blossoming into this person that I had never met before in my life. Boldness came and I thrived. I wrote a song for the young artist Katlin, we went into the studio to record and it was released. All was going well. Right? My daughter Moriah was living her dream by playing the flute and she even got to record in the studio on the track. It was good to see her smile.

A few months went by before I picked up the phone to call anyone. I was sitting on my bed one night and God pressed on my heart to call home. My pride immediately got in the way and I began to say what everyone in my family would say about me if I called home. It would just be more hurt, and I don't want that so I'll just not do that Lord. He pressed on my heart again to call home. I did. When I did, I heard the sweetest voice ever. My mom. Oh, how sweet the sound. She passed the phone to my dad, and there was another sweet sound. The sound of a man, who had missed his daughter and grand kids whom he loves dearly. We stayed on the phone and loved on each other. I was so relieved to hear from my family. I longed to see them, but the whispers in my ear were not yet. I couldn't understand why. But God had His Almighty hand in it. Things began to happen and hurt resurfaced. Wait a minute. I thought this was gone. I had forgiven and I was yet going on with life. Then God lead me into my small closet, with a bible and a flash light, as strange as it may seem, and He began to have His way. I remember crying, and crying, and crying for over an hour. You see, I had decided when I left, that I would not cry! All of that came pouring on me like a flood. I couldn't pray. I just wept before the Lord. I asked for guidance and totally surrendered what I wanted to be to Him. He began to take me on a journey called "Warriors of Praise." He let me know He saw and honored my heart towards what I was attempting to do. He saw all of it.

Then He showed me when things changed. He showed me the times where I should have stood up to the devil, but I laid down and took it. God was trying to save me from a bitter heart, but my timidness was greater than my ability to war against what the devil was trying to do to the group. Sometimes, you have to take a stand for righteousness even if you are alone. God loves a humble spirit, but there are times in your life, where you have to rise up and rebuke the enemy in an authoritative way. You have to defeat that devil on your knees and through fasting and praying. Bitterness slipped into my heart and I wasn't even aware of it until God showed me when and why I was bitter, and how not to let it happen again. He didn't point fingers and say, I saw when this happened, or when they did this, and when you did this. He chastened me, and me alone, because He expected better out of me. That was my test, and I failed it miserably. Sometimes, God will use those closest to you to put you through the refining fire. Will you be able to take it? Lord willing, yes.

The blinders had come off, and I stopped the blame game. I didn't care who did what, and why. That was no longer my problem. I let it become my problem, by the way I responded to things. Life kept going on, and I was feeling better than I had felt in a long time, but God wasn't done with me yet. He started allowing the waters to be troubled again. Please keep in mind that I had praying parents that were fasting and on their knees on my behalf. I am quite sure my sisters Jennifer and Melanie, and my grandmother Mary, and my Word of Truth Ministries family were praying as well. As a matter of fact I know they were. A couple of them called to let me know so, or reached out to me through social media to check in on us. Plus, I had new friends on my end that were sincerely praying on my behalf.

One of the people God placed in my life was Anicee. A Jamaican woman shorter than me 5'4, yet her spirit is taller than any giant. Just to look at her, you'd be a little nervous to speak. I'm not kidding. But once you get to know her, the love that this woman has for God is truly fascinating to me. She shared many stories of her life in Jamaica that taught me to keep holding on and to quit allowing the downfall of man to determine whether or not I'm going to serve God that day. Yes, I've heard that we should take our eyes off man a thousand times before her. But the way this woman talked about her Savior Jesus Christ, and no matter what we are still mere man, made from dust, it helped me to separate the man from the man of God. She spent time showing me in the word how I had to look past what I think, see, and feel. I have also witnessed her doing the things she would speak to me. Sure, we all have our flaws, but when you find someone after God's own heart, trust me, it speaks volumes! It had a great impact on my life. Now when the storms rose in life, I had a new eye sight in how I saw it. Although I don't always get it right, I still am better at recognizing the enemy a little bit swifter than before.

Once again, God started shifting things. He started moving people out of my circle, and bringing new ones in. By this time, I'm renewed. I'm hearing what the Spirit of the Lord is saying, and I'm literally watching God cause people to trip over their words that they really would rather I didn't know, people began to walk out of my life and they didn't even know why, people were moving away that had no idea that they were about to move. I didn't budge. Yes, I hurt briefly, and I do mean briefly. But I saw something they didn't see. I saw God setting the stage. He was so smooth with it, until I couldn't do anything but hold His hand through the ride and watch Him work on my behalf.

To make a long story short, when God finished working His marvelous works, I was sitting back at Word of Truth Ministries. Some may ask, why would God send you back? My answer is this. He sent me back to pass the test I failed. He sent me back because His ways are not our ways. His thoughts are not our thoughts. He is a God of peace and not the author of confusion. He sent me back to finish my season of work where it all began with this dance group. He sent me back to honor the prayer request of those who stood in the gap on my behalf. He sent me back because He wanted me to pass the test, so He could elevate me to the next level.

Now that I'm back, is everything the same? No way! We are all greater than we were before. We have all grown on different levels. Is everyone back in the group? No, but they are my biggest supporters. I love each and every last one of them even more than before. We are all sisters and when one of us feels down, we all feel the burden. When one of us have something great going on in our lives, we all share that experience.

One day I was trying to make a dance fit, that just didn't fit anymore. I was kind of ill about it, and my dad spoke something that some may think is a hard pill to swallow. But I thought of all the wisdom He's imparted to me before, and I thought this time around I'd better listen a bit more. He said, "why don't you just take the group, and start all over from the beginning." I decided to listen to his guidance. At rehearsal I told the dancers that we were going back to the basics. Let's start at the beginning. For daddy's Pastor Anniversary this year, let's dance to "Take Me To the King." Let's include our new mime team that God added to our team (which are outstanding)! Let's bring the young girls back, they want to dance, and let's give it all we have got, and let's give it all to God. They smiled with delight, and for daddy's anniversary, "Warriors of Praise" will be dancing a new dance.

I'd like to give recognition to those who have been faithful in dancing whether past or present, with "Warriors of Praise" Because of you all, I am a better person today. I thank each of you for your love, support, dedication, and allowing me to sometimes push you to the limit. May God continue to bless each and every last one of you. I love you all so much. We will always be a team, no matter where life takes us. Love, your dance teacher, Shan

Dancers:

Jennifer
Krystal
Melanie
Monique
Moriah
Tomeka

Jr. Dancers:

Jerquashia
Kelli
Maya
Montasia
Paris

Mime Team:
Quintavious
Xavier

CHAPTER 6
WHEN BROKENNESS GOES UNNOTICED
CHURCH HURT

When brokenness goes unnoticed people tend to slip through the cracks. When church hurt is not addressed people can dwindle away. You look up one day and someone is gone and everyone is wondering what happened to them. When some have gone through church hurt or any other hurt as a matter of fact, they sometimes don't know how to deal with it. They get so turned off by the church or they feel so embarrassed about their situation that they feel like they can run away from God by staying away from the church,

Church hurt is real in this day and time and if those who are leaders in the church do not adhere to the signs and voices that are calling out to them from the pews than many churches will find themselves closed. That maybe just why some of the churches in this day and time have had to close their doors because they are not seriously dealing with church hurt. People are in a dire need of serious answers for the situations and circumstances that they are in today and if the church can't be where people can come to and find that answer than they will continue to stay away. Who wants to come to a place that will tear you down when you are already feeling bad about yourself. Who wants to come to a place where the people who are supposed to be God fearing

Christians but they treat you worse than those who are in the world?

If the church cannot begin to be a source of strength and not point out someone's weaknesses than we are in trouble. The church cannot continue to allow some to misrepresent the God that we are telling them that they should serve. There has to be an accountability for the actions and the church does have to begin to mend the hurt that some of its people have caused. Now keep in mind I am not saying all churches are out to hurt or have hurt people but for those that have hurt its members or even disappointed its members there must be reconciliation.

I know for me I grew up not knowing what I wanted. Not knowing certain things and going along because it was what I was told to do. This can get many in trouble when we walk blindly and are not careful about the church. Some people tend to walk around with blinders on when it comes to their church leaders. They believe that they can do no wrong or they put them on these pedestals and when they do make mistakes they find themselves hurt and disappointed. You cannot see your church leaders as perfect church leaders because they are susceptible to making mistakes.

When you see them as humans and that they are fallible you will have a better understanding and you may be disappointed but not necessarily hurt as well. Getting past church hurt is something that I had to do and I couldn't do that until I could face that truth. When I faced that truth and saw my church for what it was and decided to deal with it, I moved on past it. Part of dealing with it meant that I had to go away from my church that I had grown up in and that my parents were attending as well. This wasn't just any church, this was my family and sometimes family can hurt you more than anyone else.

Sometimes how situations are handled can make a difference and the church has to be careful in how it handles situations with its members, especially when there is hurt involved. So, leaving my church was not an easy decision but it was one that I made and felt that had to be made at that time. Leaving made me think of the times that I had been hurt by my church, and even those times that I didn't want to be anywhere near a church. That hurt feeling that I had from years ago that had been allowed to fester and grow deep inside of me. Leaving brought me to that place that I thought I had left behind but it had suddenly or not so suddenly crept back up on me and made its way back into my thinking.

I had all kinds of thoughts that began to run through my head. I went all the way back to when I was younger and my parents not being there or seeming to not being there because of the church. How the church was not there for me and my family when we needed them and they made us feel embarrassed and humiliated. What my father was doing was for them and they couldn't even see to it that he and his family were taken care of because he was making sure that his church was being taken care of. Why didn't the church see the hurt in my eyes or in my actions when I was going through all of the difficult situations that I was going through instead of ridiculing me or laughing at me or talking about me behind my back? Why did church members who I thought were supposed to be my protectors turn out to be those who preyed on me instead of praying for me? All of these thoughts came back to me and I felt that I had to go!!

I was so broken and in order for me to get put back together again I had to do this. Here I was, this person who from the outside looking in, had it all together but that was so far from the truth. The façade had to end. The mask had to come off and the bitterness, despair and anger had to be released. Had I not left this would have never happened. In some respect I felt like I was running from church to church to church and the same things seemed to be happening. In leaving my church I found myself dealing with the same issues at other churches. There are some people who do as I did and go "church hopping" as it is sometimes called. We wonder from church to church searching for something that you can't find because you haven't dealt with the real issue and that real issue maybe you.

I know I just stepped on some toes and I had my toes stepped on too when it came to this. Going from church to church is not going to solve your issue. Your issue won't be solved until you take it to God and let him deal with you, and let him show you where you should be. When you allow that to happen you will find yourself being fed and not led in the wrong way. When you allow God to deal with the church hurt you will find yourself seeing when and if you do not belong there and you can move on without any remorse.

Leaving my church did more than just hurt me it also hurt my family and some of the other things that I had helped to build at the church, one being the dance group. When we deal with church hurt sometimes we don't think about anything or anyone but ourselves and that is not wrong. You must put your well-being before anyone else's. Some may not understand it but you must do what you have to do in order to get back to your wholeness. Trust God to direct you and believe that it will be ok. There are some who deal with church hurt in different ways but the only way to deal with it is to let God deal with it.

The church is a hospital for the spiritually sick and just like in a hospital you must be diagnosed and given the proper medicine if you are to get well. Some have been mis-diagnosed in the church and there are some who need to go and get a second opinion about their diagnosis. The only person that knows if they have been mis-diagnosed is you. You must take the time to evaluate what your doctor(Pastor) is telling you and do your own research, which is read the bible for yourself and develop your own relationship with God. God will not mis-diagnose you. He will not mislead you or misdirect you. He will take care of you and get you back to being whole. Anyone who is not trying to get you back to wholeness is someone that is not after God's own heart and you should not be listening to them. Whether that person is family, friend, spouse or boyfriend/girlfriend, you need to put yourself as far away from them as possible.

Church hurt can be direct or indirect. I think that I have had to deal with both sides of that coin. I have been hurt directly and indirectly. There is no need to rehash some of the events again or situations but when you have church hurt and don't deal with it, you cause yourself to suffer spiritually and emotionally sometimes longer than you should. Part of getting back from broken for me was dealing with my church hurt. That hurt caused me to lose some things and even some relationships. I am a firm believer that sometimes in order to gain we sometimes must lose. I know it doesn't make sense but trust me one day it will. In losing sometimes we gain a greater understanding that we might not have gotten had we not lost what it was that God didn't intend for us to keep.

Church hurt is real and sometimes we are hurt by the religious aspect of the church as well. When you are in a vulnerable state or even in a young state of mind you don't fully understand what is right and what is wrong. The church has done and can do damage to people's way of looking at church just in the way that they teach the word of God. The manipulation of the word can do irreparable damage to people so church leaders please be careful in how you bring forth the word of God and how you instruct the people of God. Some can be so stringent that we hold people's minds captive and confine them to an unrealistic standard that not even you can live up to.

Yes, God wants us to heed his word and to live according to his word but no one wants to be made to feel as if they are going directly to Hell if they do one thing wrong. Leaders; please be careful to not only talk about the God of wrath but also talk about the God of Love and forgiveness. God is not just someone that beats us or scolds us, he is a God that loves us and wants us to be who he has predestined us to be. If we only know a God of wrath or a God that hurts than we are misleading people about who God really is. I had to learn that there was more to God than just those who mis-represented him and wanted to use his name in order to extract something from me. I had to learn that everyone that used God's name did not truly know who God was.

It wasn't until I began to get back to talking with God and spending time with God that I understood who God was. We will never know all there is to know about God because who he is is infinite but the more time that I spent with him the more the church hurt began to go away because I began to get to know him. The way that you get over church hurt is by running to God not away from God. Let me say that again, the way that we get over church hurt is by running to God not away from God. I chose to run from God in the beginning. Just like Jonah, in the bible, when God told him to go to Nineva, he ran. He didn't want any part of what God was telling him to do. Just like the Prodigal son, who wanted all of what was his right then, he ran. And just like them I ran.

What these people found out, just like I found out was that no matter where you run to God is there. He was with Jonah when he tried to run on the boat, he was with the Prodigal son when he came to himself in the pigpen and he was with me when I tried to run from church to church to church. YOU CAN'T OUT RUN GOD!!!! The sooner we get that the better. Running from God is not going to make the church hurt or any other kind of hurt go away. So what I need you to do is plant both of your feet firmly on the floor, stand squared up and declare that you will not run anymore!!!! That hurt that you were feeling is gone, that bitterness that came from that Pastor that you put up on a pedestal and he/she let you down is gone. That church member that said something about you that you know was a lie is over and done with. That relationship that you had in the church that everybody knows about; doesn't matter anymore. The church hurt has got to go!!!

I believe that if the church would address the hurt of its members instead of sometimes giving people what they may want to hear, there would be less church hurt. I think that when people have a false perception of dealing with issues their expectations of the church are made greater. I believe that there needs to be a reality check in the church so that people in the church understand what God wants from us. I think that when the church truly heeds the word of God the leaders of that church or the church as a whole will lead those who are hurting to the one who can give them their wholeness back again.

Isn't that or shouldn't that be the goal of the church to lead all those who are weary and heavy laden to the one that can give them rest. If you as a church leader are not leading your congregants to the one that sets them free, you are hurting them. Remember earlier in the chapter I said that the church is a hospital for the spiritually sick, well when you are spiritually sick or mentally sick or physically sick you don't go to someone that is going to make it worse, we go to someone who is going to make it better. If you as a church leader are not making people better than what are you doing?

So, now that I have given you the bad side of church hurt let's get to how to make it better.

You begin to heal church hurt by first admitting that you were hurt. The first way that you solve a problem is by first admitting that you have a problem. By admitting that you were hurt you say to yourself, what am I hurting from? You must get to the root of your hurt and begin to see how and why you were hurt. Was it someone in the church that hurt me, or was it something about the church that I was hurting from? As you dive into this question you will begin to understand yourself better and you can better deal with what or who hurt you.

Once you have admitted the hurt than you must look at yourself first and see what part you played in the hurt. I know this is not going to be easy as it was not easy for me either, but you must do it!!!It is necessary for you to understand your responsibility in why you may be hurting. You may bear no responsibility but you will not know if you do not take a look at yourself and analyze you. There is an old saying that when you point one finger at someone there are three pointing back at you. There is a reason for that and that reason is that before we blame others for our hurt we must first see what part of the hurt that we are accountable for.

After you have held yourself accountable you then can look at others and see what part they played in the hurt that you are going through. To many of us want to jump straight to this part and skip over the self-analysis. Well, that is not going to happen here because we are on our journey to wholeness and in order to be whole we have to look at the full picture. We must see what part we played in this situation as well as the part that others played in the situation. This part is not the blame game and we have to understand that getting to the hurt has a reason and a purpose. The reason is forgiveness and the purpose is to be whole again. Did you get that….the reason you see what part a person played in the situation is to forgive them and the purpose for forgiveness is to be whole again. You cannot get to wholeness without forgiveness!!! I just said something right there, so let me remind you of it again. YOU CANNOT GET TO WHOLENESS WITHOUT FORGIVENESS!!!!

As I have said throughout the book, I had to forgive. I not only had to forgive myself, I had to forgive those who had hurt me. I don't think that we realize that we do hurt ourselves. We can hurt ourselves by the choices that we make and sometimes even the situations that we put ourselves in. At the end of the day all forgiveness must begin with yourself. I want you to start by saying that right now to yourself, I FORGIVE YOU….I FORGIVE YOU…I FORGIVE YOU!!! When you can forgive yourself you can begin to get back from broken.

Now that you have forgiven yourself you must now work on forgiving those who have hurt you. It took me some time to work through this but I can finally say that I have gotten to that place and that those who have hurt me I have forgiven them. I talked about this in previous chapters and I meant what I said about truly forgiving the people in my past that have hurt me. I can say that because I forgave me first. When you begin to forgive you will put yourself in a place where you can move forward and you no longer suffer from the church hurt that once held you back from getting to your wholeness.

CHAPTER 7
BITTERNESS....THE BLACK HOLE

The definition of bitterness is anger and disappointment for being treated unfairly, resentment. Bitterness is a black hole. It is a setup for a set-back. It is a stranglehold to keep you from growing spiritually. Bitterness can be very tricky. You can be around people that you have bitter feelings towards. You can go out to dinner with someone you are bitter with and you can even have a conversation with someone that you hold bitter feelings towards. The strength of bitterness can be overwhelming if you allow it to dwell and fester on the inside.

Bitterness has many faces. It is a deep black hole that any of us can fall into. If you are holding in any bitter feelings towards anyone than you need to take a deep look at yourself and understand the feelings that you are allowing yourself to hold onto. You know the truth and how you feel if a person that you are holding ill feelings towards walks in a room. People can do so many evil things to you that can make you feel resentment or anger towards them but you are the one that controls your feelings not them.

You must understand that the only one that controls your feelings and actions is you. If you give someone that kind of power over your life, than you really must search within yourself and evaluate where you are in your feelings. Bitterness is a black hole that one can fall into very quickly. If you are not careful you can find yourself "slippin into darkness", as the group War use to sing. We can become so consumed by the hate, anger and bitterness that we feel that it becomes a way of life for us. There are many people today who are walking around holding bitterness in from their childhoods. They have yet to let go of how they were mistreated by their mother or how their father was never there for them. Our society has become a bunch of pint up time bombs that can go off at any moment.

There are many who still suffer the bitterness of a bad relationship or maybe even two. They continue to hold onto these bitter past feelings and allow them to pile on throughout relationships and never deal with the issues and as a consequence you have these broke people dealing with broke people and even broke people reproducing with broke people and raising someone who grows into a broke and bitter person. The cycle can continue if this bitterness is not dealt with. We have to understand that forgiveness is a way to get out of the bitterness black hole. If there was anyone who had the right to be bitter and angry it was Jesus Christ himself. He dealt with people who criticized him, ridiculed him, hated him, tried to kill him and even betrayed him. In spite of all that he went through he held no bitterness or anger towards anyone.

The fact of the matter is even while hanging on the cross he said; "father, forgive them for they know not what they do." Wow, that is such a powerful statement and the blueprint for all of us and how we should deal with bitterness. Now, I know none of us are perfect and we may not be quite at that point yet but the point is for us to always be striving to get to that point and not let that bitterness and anger stay inside of us and never deal with it. It's not worth it. I have been through a lot in my life time. I can't even begin to tell it all in this book nor do I think I will talk about certain things but none the less I will say this, I LET IT GO!!! When you have truly dealt with something, bitterness, anger, resentment, all of those ill feelings that you have been holding inside, you don't even wish to go back there and say anything more about it. It has been let go and therefore can no longer do what it used to do to you. Once I let it go I began to see things differently. I began to feel differently. The burdens that I use to hold onto no longer had the effect on me that they once did. I became a new me. I rose from the black hole of bitterness and emerged victorious over it.

It took me a while to get here, so don't think that you will get over this feeling over-night. It is a process and a gradual progression into wholeness. That is what you must remember throughout this whole process. The goal is wholeness and wholeness is a process. See yourself advancing through the process. As you deal with it you will see your growth and eventually you will see the changes that have taken place in you and how you handle different situations. God will use the people and situations to help you to grow. He will use these situations to get out of you what he wants to get out of you.

When you don't allow God to get out of you what he wants to get out of you through people or situations that have hurt you, you stunt your growth. You don't allow yourself to become who it is that you are supposed to become. You will find yourself taking the same test over and over and over again until God gets out of you what he wants out of you. Once you have learned the lesson than you will be able to move on and you will be the better person for it. You will have gotten to the point where what you have been through has no bearing on who you are and where you are going.

Declare peace in your life and begin to walk in that peace and move out of the black hole that you were once in. Begin to allow God to heal and purify your heart so that you no longer look and feel the way that you once did. Don't go around trying to justify being bitter and you have no right to hold onto that bitterness, but if you let go he will let go. I know that you may be hurting and it may seem impossible to let go but let me give you a word of encouragement right here, you CAN do, you MUST do it and you WILL do it because your life depends on it. Let that bitterness go and let it know that it has no power over you. Let it know that it's time inside of you has expired. Let it know that the lease is up and it has to be gone right now!!!! It cannot pass go, it cannot collect two hundred dollars, right now, it must be gone!!!!

Be filled with the love that Jesus felt on the cross and was able to walk through the battle of bitterness and come out on the other side feeling renewed and whole. Turn away from the bitterness and the hurt because it is not worth it. We want to blame everybody but ourselves for our bitterness but ourselves. The only real person that we need to look at is ourselves. They say that when you point a finger at someone you have three pointing back at you. Why do you think that is? It means that we need to look at ourselves before we can point a finger at anyone else.

That bitterness that's inside of you is keeping you from shining and showing others that they cannot and will not hold you back. When you let the bitterness go you show others how they can be whole too. You show them that they too have the power to get out of the black hole of bitterness. What kind of person do you think will believe you are whole and following the God you serve if you allow yourself to constantly show an attitude of bitterness, anger and resentment? They will say what God is it that she or he serves because I certainly don't want to follow them. Think of the example that you are setting when you have let that bitterness go and you heap hot coals over those who once hurt you and thought they had gotten the best of you.

You are supposed to be the prime example of what others who are going through can become. Set the example, set the tone, set the standard. Everything that I am telling you to do I had to do. I was a sickly person holding onto the bitterness and using every excuse in the book to justify my feelings. I walked around spewing my venom at anyone that got in my path. I was mean and judgmental all because of what I had been through and I wanted to blame everyone for it. I had no energy and my heart was hardened and looking for pity from everywhere and everyone. It wasn't until I decided to get on my knees and deal with my issues with the God that I serve I was then able to move forward. The harshness and the bitterness began to fall away. We must be real with ourselves and deal with it because if we don't then

God will deal with us and by that time it will be to late.

There are somethings that we must deal with and begin to get pass. You must understand that your parents were not perfect that Uncle that may have hurt you is not perfect or that cousin that was your best friend growing up that hurt you is not perfect. That boyfriend or girlfriend that you felt betrayed by is not perfect. Getting beyond that hurt is where your wholeness lies and that is where I am trying to get you to in reading this book. Begin to see yourself whole again. Begin to see yourself on the other side of through. It is there but you must push through until you get there.

It is amazing that I had to have children in order to figure all of this out. It's time to be grown and face responsibility and that's what I had to face when I had my children. Let your light shine so that others may be able to be led from the black hole of bitterness. Let go, let go, let go and push your way through that storm that you may be going through. As you go further and further you will get stronger and stronger and with each passing day you become more and more whole. Through all of the bitterness and darkness God has not left you and that is his promise to you that he would never leave you nor forsake you. Move in your purpose, move in your greatness and become that victorious person you are called to be.

I know it may be painful and hurtful but I promise you if you deal with it you will heal, you will get through and you will smile again, you will feel joy again. You will get to the point again where those that have hurt you in the past have no effect on you and you can even deal with them in a pleasant manner and not feel the bitterness that you once felt. I even had someone that I was deeply hurt by contact me through social media and I was able to deal with them because I had dealt with my bitterness and I no longer allowed that hurt to be my bondage.

He went into the reasons why he did what he did and I found myself thinking about his words and what he said. He thought that it would be difficult for me to forgive him for what had taken place but what he did not know was that God had already dealt with me and I had already forgiven him years ago. After a little while I let him know that I had forgiven him years ago and that I was no longer holding onto what was done. He was in shock as to what I made him aware of and couldn't believe that I had forgiven him. He had in his mind that I was still bitter about what had happened and therefore took all this time to contact me and ask for forgiveness.

Isn't that the same way that we do with God ourselves. We find ourselves doing something that we feel we shouldn't have done and we feel ashamed about it with God so we turn away from him and think that he will not forgive us for it when all the time he was waiting for us to come to him and recognize that he had already forgiven us. Well, it took me some time to get that lesson to but now that I got it I want you to get it too. Get it that you are already forgiven and no matter what you think he has already forgiven you. You can go to him, you can believe in him because IT IS FORGIVEN!!!!

Nothing that we do is free but here is the good thing, Jesus paid it all!!! I told you about my ex-husband who searched and searched for me and when he connected with me and was astonished when I told him that I had forgiven him years and years ago. What are we teaching our children, what are we teaching each other when we hold onto the bitterness and stay in that black hole and walk in the hurt, walk in the anger and walk in the disappointment? When you can finally be free from all of these things you can finally fly and flourish as you are supposed to and break the strangle hold but you can't do that until you LET.....IT.....GO!!!!

CHAPTER 8
FINDING HEALING IN FORGIVENESS

So here I am broken, broken and away from my family. I am seriously toe up from the flo up.
I am here and I am here all alone. At least I felt alone. I did have some friends but in the state that I was in I didn't realize what that friendship meant. When you are broken and trying to find healing you must surround yourself with people who are willing to walk with you through your healing. I was blessed to have some very good friends who were willing to not help me through but to be honest enough with me to let me know the things that I needed to deal with, heal from and confront.

Part of that confrontation was coming to terms with the way that I left. In our trials sometimes we don't get things right the first time. The trial/test is there to move us into the direction that God intends for us to go in. It may take us a few times to pass the test but you will not move forward until you get out of the test what it is that God needs for you to get from it. Part of my test was dealing with the way that I left. I had to make it right and I would not be able to deal with healing and moving forward until I dealt with this issue.

I'm here and I am going on and doing some great things. I had written a song that was successful and had been released on Itunes and various other outlets but to look at me you would think that everything was great. My family was doing well; kids are accomplishing great things and doing well in school. In spite of all of this there was still the feeling of emptiness. I found myself up at 2 o'clock in the morning one time and I went onto Youtube. I came across this guy and I hear him talk about forgiveness in a way that I had never heard it talked about before. I found myself lying on my bed thinking about what I had just heard and began to talk to the Lord and say; *"Lord, everybody that has hurt me I forgive them and anyone that I have hurt, please let them forgive me."* As soon as I finished uttering those words; it was as if I felt them from a place that I had never gone to before. I had never felt this way before. I felt it in my heart and all I could say in that moment was, I forgive you, I forgive you, I forgive you!!!!

I knew from that moment on that I was set free from the bondage of unforgiveness. I was free to begin the healing that needed to be done in my life in order to get me back from broken. See often times we do not get to the place of true healing and that place is where the hurt that we have lies. Many of us do not want to face it because we are too afraid of what we feel will be the result of what comes from that truth. When we allow ourselves to deal with our truth in being broken we come to understand what broke us and we are able to learn how to heal the brokenness and then move forward in our lives.

If you have not gotten to the point that you can say that "I FORGIVE YOU" or "I FORGIVE MYSELF" you have to figure out what you need to do in order to get to that place. I don't care if you have to cry about it. I don't care if you have to talk to someone about it or if you have to holla, scream and shout it out of you but you must GO THERE!!! Trust me once you go there and deal with it you will feel like a great weight has been lifted off of you. Also, you must allow God to walk with you through the healing. He will comfort you, he will nurture you and he will guide you every step of the way so that all that you have had to deal with gets dealt with up until that point and you can break the stoppage that has been keeping you from getting back to broken.

There are to many of us who are walking around and not getting to that healing place that we need to get to. We are walking around bitter and angry and holding onto feelings and situations that happened years ago and we won't let go of them. Forgiveness is the beginning of the healing process and the healing process leads us to wholeness. We can get there but we must renew our minds and begin to let go of all the hurt and forgive those who have done us wrong and even forgive ourselves for what we may have done wrong.

I want those of you who are reading this right now to understand this....FORGIVENESS IS NOT FOR THEM, IT IS FOR YOU!!!! When you forgive someone it is not to let the person who hurt you off the hook or to give them a pass for what they did to you. It is to get you to a place of healing. Healing cannot take place until you forgive. After I fell asleep and woke up the next morning, after my epiphany, I was filled with so much energy. It was as if this big burden had been lifted off of my shoulders. I know some of you who have gotten to the place of forgiveness can relate to this. Once you forgive you become free. You become free to think, free to live, free to be you again and free to heal!!!

My energy level was on high and I knew that it was something different because I was severely anemic and suffered from hyper thyroid. I was very, very, very tired all the time. I had learned to operate life in this tired state with no physical energy but when I woke up that morning it was different. I had also heard or read that healing is in forgiveness. I had found what I was looking for, the healing in my forgiveness.

Have you found your healing? Have you found that place that will begin to move you back from broken? Your healing is waiting on you. It is waiting on you to let go of those things that have held you captive for so long. Begin to release the experiences and issues that can no longer keep you from your happiness. Let your journey begin to move on the other side of the pain and get you to your wholeness.

I want to encourage you. I want to be a light that shows you how to shine. I want you to say if she can do it so can I. The truth be told, you have everything within you that you need in order to get you out of that place. It's time that we talk about healing and forgiveness and what is on our minds and begin to move in and through people. In the church in our homes, it's time!!! It's time for healing just like the woman with the issue of blood. It's time to begin to look at one another and understand that we can be each other's strength. We as the church need to be the place that people can come to and see the manifestation of the healing of forgiveness. The church should be and needs to be that place that someone, anyone can be uninhibited in showing their hurt and receive the tools that are needed in order to get to that healing place and move from forgiveness into their greatness.

Our churches should not be a place that people come to and feel more ashamed of what they have been through then they get at any other place that they may go to. We are the church so we set the example for those who are hurting and for those who need healing but are not sure how to get to it. We should be able to talk in such a way that people see us and they understand that we have been where they are and that they can get through it because we have gotten through it. There is nothing more powerful than those who can testify to others who are hurting and struggling with forgiveness and can show them how they begin to breakdown those walls and start to become a new person.

Our cities are filled with hurt people and it is our responsibility to get up, stand up and take someone else by the hand and show someone else how to get to the healing. Your relationships are looking for healing, your friendships are looking for healing, your families are looking for healing. What are you waiting for, it's right there for you and all you have to do is begin to move in your healing. You must begin to see those things that are right in front of you and pour into yourself and get what it is that God has for you. Your strength is growing and your healing has begun.

I am not just saying these things to you just to be saying them. I am telling you what I know and what I am dealing with and what I have dealt with. Putting all the pieces together takes time. It is not going to happen in a day, in a week or maybe not even in a year. It will happen in its own time. The thing that we must do is stay the course. My story of healing includes my children and understanding that I am so proud of each and every one of them. They are truly my blessing and make me so proud to be there mother. While the story behind my dear beloved son is not a pleasant one, as he was born of a married man, the situation happened and had to happen because of how I was and how I treated others who had gone through the same experience. I had to be humbled and broken in order that I might see me for that person that I was and how I was treating others.

Now I have more compassion for those in those kinds of situations and even other situations because of the brokenness that I had been through. Being unmerciful and unforgiving can cause you to enter into situations and circumstances that are used to humble you and give you a spirit of forgiveness. Some may feel that you don't want another relationship due to all the hurt that you had been through. You tell yourself that you would rather remain in your broken state then to allow someone else to hurt you again, but what you don't realize is that if you remain in that broken state you can only operate out of that brokenness and when you operate out of that brokenness you operate out of your hurt.

You operate out of that hurt and you not only hurt yourself you hurt others. Your bitterness and hurt won't allow you to get close to anyone. I know this because I was that way. I didn't want anyone to get close enough to me to hurt me again. I didn't want anyone to get close enough to me to be able to disappoint me again. I had been through enough of it and I didn't want to go through it again. But then, then just like the prodigal son, and I will say prodigal daughter, I came to myself and realized that the hurt and brokenness was no place for me to be. I had to leave it and all that it had taken me through behind.

You make wrong choices and you may make wrong decisions while everyone decides to put their mouth on you and judge you for the decisions that you have made. They can't see your brokenness through the decisions that you have made nor can they see the hurt that is crying out for healing but God sees it. He sees every struggle, every tear, every ache and every decision for what it is. Understand he doesn't look at the physical he looks at our hearts. He looks at our hearts and knows and understands everything that has gone on and everything that is going on with us.

God sees it and he begins to work in and through us if we allow him. Let me say that again, IF WE ALLOW HIM!!! When we allow him to get to us and get us to get to that place of forgiveness he will begin to deal with the hurt and begin the healing. I didn't understand this until I had to go to that place and allow him to deal with me and deal with it. That's when I realized where my healing was, it was in the Forgiveness!!!! Forgive somebody today. Forgive someone for the things that they may have done to you. Forgive yourself and in that forgiveness you will truly find HEALING!!!!

CHAPTER 9
REDEFINING THE WOMAN INSIDE

This chapter is near and dear to my heart. As I begin to write and talk about redefining the woman inside, a slight smile comes over my face and my heart begins to become filled with joy. I begin to feel this because this has been my motto ever since I was a in my twenties. I was told by someone years ago, after talking about a situation with them, you have to redefine the woman inside. I thought about it, and I had to think about what I had just heard. I said to myself; *Did I hear her correctly, did she just say I had to redefine the woman inside?"* After thinking for a second, I thought, wow, I had never been told that before. It struck something inside of me.

How in the world do you redefine everything that I have ever known? How do I take my DNA and change it. I searched for years for the answer and I tried to grasp what I had been told and I tried to understand what I needed to do in order to break this mindset that I had been in for years. I tried to understand how I was supposed to take everything that I had learned as a child and totally redefine it. How could I take an old way of thinking and begin to think in a totally new manner?

Well, it took some years but recently I have begun to understand what that statement meant to me. I began to realize that I couldn't change my DNA but I could change the way that I thought and the way that I was seeing things. In order for me to begin to understand this statement I had to first begin with redefining and understanding my relationship with my Lord and Savior Jesus Christ. If I was going to make a mindset change it was going to begin and end with him. When you see him from this perspective you come to know and understand that you are not a failure, you are not a lost cause, you are not what others try and define you to be. You are not a cheater, a bad mother, a whore or any other negative character that the enemy will try and get you to believe that you are.

What you are is a daughter of the most high and a child of the King. You belong to him and everything that you went through, every trial that you had to go through he was there with you every step of the way. He wants to put you back together and welcome you with open arms, you just have to do like the Prodigal son did and come to yourself and redefine who you are and understand that what he has for you is greater than what anyone has tried to tell you that you couldn't be.

Each time that I came back my Dad and my mom welcomed me back with open arms and lovingly embraced me, mistakes and all. You must begin to love yourself and the woman/man that you are. If you do not love yourself than no one else can be expected to love you. Redefining the woman inside means becoming comfortable with that woman and who she is and who she is becoming in life. There was a time when that was not possible for me because of the state of mind that I was in. Part of getting back from broken is putting the inside together. Many people try and mask themselves on the outside and are still broken on the inside. When you begin with putting the inside back together first the outside will come together, it's just a matter of time.

You must love what God sees in you. You cannot allow yourself to be defined by others because you will lose yourself every time. You will spend more time trying to please them instead of pleasing God and yourself. Your number one mistake is listening to what others say or think about you. God loves you and is crazy about you. He will take care of you and nurture you if you allow him to be who he is supposed to be in your life. Many times we get impatient or we get caught up in our own thing that we forget that it is not who we are as ourselves but who God wants us to be. When we stray away from who he wants us to be we find ourselves in the proverbial pig pen having to "come to ourselves."

I know there are many of you who have had those "come to yourself" moments. In order to get back from broken those "come to yourself" or ah ha moments as Ms. Oprah Winfrey calls them, must happen to us. The redefining the woman inside begins at that Ah ha moment. You begin to see things in a new and different way. You begin to see yourself not as a failure but as a conqueror, not as a loser but as a winner and not as a victim but as the victor!!! It all starts at the Ah ha!!!

When you get to the ah ha moment you begin to see the people for who they are and the relevance that they play in your life. You will begin to see that there are some individuals who will be left behind because they cannot go with you on your journey back to wholeness. There are also those who will be along with you and will be there to assist you along the way. Whether it is a significant other, a close friend, or even family members, there will be those who God places in your space to assist you on your journey so appreciate them for the love that they have to give you and the love that they offer to you. There love is a part of that healing process and will help you to begin to see what true love looks like and what it feels like.

Redefining the woman inside also involves allowing yourself to be open to who you will become. You have to take the time to chip away at the hard pieces and get to the core of that woman, build on that foundation. You have to be willing to tell the truth about what and who you were. It wasn't pretty and it certainly didn't look good when I reflect on the state that I was in. I was in relationships that I knew I had no business being in, It was at that point that I began to understand that God was with me and never left me. As I look back I began to get stronger because I was allowing God to be my protector and my guide back to wholeness.

We must begin to encourage one another and not tear one another down. When we see someone in the broken state we must be strong enough to reach out and let them know that they can get back from broken. Part of the purpose of why I have written this book is so that other women can see what I have been through and know that they can do what I have done and get to that place that I call WHOLENESS!!!! When we begin to redefine the woman inside we start to stand tall and understand the state that we were once in and that you know who you are, you have substance, you have power, you have worth and authority over you and no one but God is over you.

It's a beautiful thing when you begin to redefine the woman inside because you begin to shine from the inside out and you not only do that for yourself you begin to give others permission to do the same and to give them hope that they to can shine again. You set the example for them and they have that mark that they can aspire to and not allow society to define who they are. They will no longer let magazines define who they are, they will no longer let social media define who they are and they will not let anyone else define them. The atmosphere begins to change when you redefine the woman inside.

Redefining myself from the inside has not been easy and I have not always liked it but despite that I keep moving and keep going. I may have failed today but I will not fail tomorrow and even if I fall or fail I will get back up, dust myself off and keep moving forward. I cannot define myself without defining myself in who God is to me. Will there be times that I doubt me, yes, will there be days that the struggle is more than others, yes, will there be days that I wish this refinement was over with, of course. But what I also know is whose I am and who is within me and that is enough to get me through and keep me on the journey of redefining myself.

When you start to redefine the woman inside you begin to get and gather the peace from within and you know that money can't give you peace. The friendships don't make you, your spouse doesn't make you, material things don't make you. The car, the house, jewelry, none of those things make you who you are. You stop lying to yourself and all the others that you think are looking at you. You begin to stand up and know that you are a light shining to show others how to get to the true light and perhaps keep them from going through what you went through. You will declare that you are the daughter of the King, the one who made you Beautiful and Wonderfully. There will be no doubt that when you begin to redefine the woman inside; you begin to take on a new persona and that new persona will affect and effect those who are around you. You will see that people will see you differently, people will talk to you different all because of the commanding presence that has come from within. Don't let anyone DEFINE THE WOMAN INSIDE BUT GOD!!!!

CHAPTER 10
BACK FROM BROKEN

I think that this title is self- explanatory. No, I am by no means perfect. I have flaws and I am still working on the person that I am to become. When I say back from broken I mean that person you were before you were broken. Broken, hopeless and feeling as if you cannot get up again. That feeling that you might have had that had you believing that there was no way things were going to get better. That state of mind that had you so wrapped up that you believed the lie that you were less than. I am talking about being in a place that your circle of friends said uh uh, we gettin you out of this and they just begin to pray for you.

That back from broken feeling is the best. When you go through so much and still smile. That back from broken feeling that has you going through a bad day and take it just for that and not see it as a bad life. When you can forgive someone and truly mean it, that's being back from broken. That moment that all the hurt, shame, bitterness and anger has been released from you and it no longer controls you, that is being back from broken. This book has taken you on a journey and hopefully in this last chapter you have gotten to the point where you understand what it takes to get to this point right here. You have dealt with all of your emotions, feelings and anxieties and you are now ready to say all the pieces are together and I am moving forward into my back from broken state of mind. I need for you to get this. In order for you to get through to the finish line that is in front of you, you must be willing to push like you have never pushed yourself before.

There will be those who criticize you for this new mindset that you have now. There will be some that will say that you have changed. Let them know, yes, I have changed, I have changed for the better because, I am back from broken. The person that I use to be, I no longer am. That person that you knew is no longer who I am. You are stronger than you have ever been before. You are greater than you have ever been before. By no means are you finished. Now is just the beginning. You have just put it all together and now the real work begins.

I am ending this book but by no means is my journey over. I want women all across the globe to know what it feels like to be back from broken. I want you all to know that you can put the pieces back together again. You can be whole again. Your relationship with God is whole and now all of your other relationships will take on the same form. You are equipped, you are prepared, you are ready for anything that may come against you. Do not be afraid to face anything that comes against you because you are covered.

Wholeness is a state of mind. Are you going to make mistakes and fall again, yes, but the difference between the person you were and the person that you are now is that you will dust yourself off and get back up and keep it moving. You have moved from bitterness and hurt to now completion and wholeness. This journey that you have come through is for a purpose. Be encouraged and know that you are better because of all of it. I know that it may not seem like it but you are better. I hope that by reading this book that you have been able to see yourself and how you can walk through this journey of brokenness into wholeness and become who it is that you are meant to be. Greatness is your calling and it is up to you whether or not you answer.

No one is going to force you to believe in you. No one is going to always be there to encourage you so you will sometimes have to do what David did and encourage yourself. It may seem sometimes like you are walking through your journey all by yourself but know that you are never alone. Surround yourself with those that will encourage you when you need it. Surround yourself with those who are heading in the same positive direction that you are heading in. It is important that you get yourself an accountability partner. This is someone that will not tell you what you want to hear but what you need to hear.

I need for you to prepare yourself for the next battle that you will face by surrounding yourself with battle warriors!!! Your battle warriors are those individuals that will not only fight with you they will fight for you. When you get weary and may feel a little down, they will be there to fight for you. When your back is up against the wall they will be right there with you every step of the way and will not leave your side. The word tells us that the battle is not given to the swift nor the strongest but it is given to him/her that endureth til the end. Your battle warriors will be there with you til the end.

Now that you have gotten your battle warriors in your corner with you there needs to be a battle plan so that when you encounter the enemy of bitterness again you are prepared. No General goes into battle without a battle plan. Your battle plan should include reading your word on a daily basis. Not only should you be in your word on a daily basis you need to be talking with your Commander-In-Chief, who is God, about how you are going to handle your day. You should never go into a battle without speaking with your Commander-In-Cheif(God) first. He will lead you and guide you in the direction that he wants you to go in.

Now that you are whole again the enemy will do everything in his power to get you back to that place of brokenness again so you must always be on your guard. He is not going anywhere. He may have retreated for the moment but you better believe that he is coming back again. This time when he comes back you will be ready. You will be ready because you have seen his playbook before and you understand what he will try to do and you are ready.

Now that you have your warriors with you and you have got your word in you and the Commander has covered you, you now must handle the task of being who you are called to be. You must be strong, you must be powerful, you must be relentless and you must be purposeful in everything that you do. Getting back from broken is not just something that you say it is something that you live. You live each day putting one foot in front of the other handling the ups and downs that life will throw at you.

You have made it back from broken so now it is your responsibility to assist someone else to get there. You have to become someone's source of guidance out of the darkness of bitterness into the light of wholeness. You have to understand that everything that you went through was not just so you could go through it, learn from it and keep the lessons to yourself. You went through so that what you learned you could teach to someone else so they could get through as well. Understand that what you went through is bigger than just you. It was not meant for just you. You have been equipped and now you must equip.

This journey that I have been on has been one of trials, triumphs and testimonies. The trials taught me not only who I was but it also taught me whose I was. I can now say to you that I am a woman of God who is whole and knows that my Father loves me and cares for me. I can not only say that to myself but I can say that to you. He loves you and cares for you as well. My trials also showed me how tough I was. I didn't know my strength until I had endured some of the things that I had to go through. My trials brought out the best in me. They brought out a strength that I did not know I had in me and because of that I am even stronger than I ever thought I could be.

My triumphs taught me that I have victory. I am an overcomer. I can be successful when I focus and I am in tune with what my purpose is. There were times that I didn't think that I would be where I am today but there was something inside of me that kept me going and I know that you can and will do the same. Your triumphs are there to give you encouragement. They are there to remind you that getting through to wholeness is achievable but you just have to keep going. You keep going not because you want to but you keep going because you have to. There is always that piece of you that is deep down inside of you that will not let you quit. That little piece of you remembers when you made it through a certain situation that you know you had no idea how you were going to get through. It's that piece of you that remembers when people counted you out and told you that you would not be able to do it but look at you now. You have become what others said that you would never be again!!!

This third piece that keeps you going is your testimony. Your testimony is not so that you can make it but it is so that someone else can make it. Don't ever let an opportunity go by without letting someone know that if you can make they can too. They need to hear your story; they need to know that even though they may be in the pit right now there is a palace waiting for them. Let them know that between the pit and the palace there will be days and nights of crying and asking why. There will be days of heart wrenching hurt and bitterness but you will get through it. You must let them know that if they faint not the palace is there for them. You must let them know that the palace was not for you but it is for those who will need you. They will need you in order for them to get through their journey.

The great thing about my testimony is that it is designed to make life better for you and your testimony is designed to make life better for someone else. You have read this book up to this point and hopefully I have said something that has resonated in your soul and will lift you when you are down, carry you when you maybe weary and comfort you when you feel discouraged. This book was designed to be my hand extending to you to help you get up, move forward and move into your rightful place of greatness. My hand is out there for you and all you have to do is reach out for it, grab it and pull yourself up.

I hope that what you have read has given you strength, encouragement and excitement for what is about to happen in your life. Do know that the joy that I am feeling as I write this is the joy that you will feel too. You have no choice in the matter because once you have gotten Back From Broken you cannot do anything but smile and be glad that you have let go of everything that once had a hold on you.

Your days of anger are over, your days of bitterness are over, your days of being the tail and not the head are through!!!! You are a mighty child of God and you can begin to act like it. Don't hold back and you cannot hold it in, release it and be who you are called to be. You are whole again and there is nothing that can break you. If you ever feel as if you are slipping back into that bitterness hole again you can pick this book up and begin to go back and read it until you feel your strength coming back again. You will not be defeated. YOU CANNOT LOSE!!!

Now that I have enlightened you, taught you what you needed to know and I have empowered you, which is equipped you with the tools that you need in order to walk in your wholeness, the last thing that I hope that I can do for you is to impact you. I hope that I have impacted you in such a way that you can go out and be who it is that you are purposed to be and do the same as I have done for you. It doesn't have to be in the form of a book. It doesn't have to be in the form of teaching or preaching but all it has to be is a word to someone, a hand up to someone or even telling someone about what you have made it through. I charge you to believe in someone so much so that they believe that they can become who it is that you are becoming and they see in themselves what I see in you. You are that great woman, you are that great man, you are destined for greatness and don't let anybody tell you who you can't become. The bitterness has been laid to rest, the anger has been cast aside and you are free to be healed. You have become whole again because you have made it **BACK FROM BROKEN!!!!**

AFTERWORD

YES, I SURVIVED!!

BACK FROM BROKEN

By no means am I perfect. I still
have flaws and areas that I am working
on. When I say back from broken I don't
mean this perfect person. What I mean is
who you are before you discover who you
are. That me I was when all the pieces had
to be put back together again.
Broken, hopeless, down and out, that feeling
you have of falling down and never being
able to get back up again.
That back from broken feeling is the best
because it's a feeling that no one can take
from you. It's the feeling of going through
so much and still be able to smile. You have
an understanding that there will be bad
days but it does not mean that you have a bad
life. When you can forgive and truly mean it
from your heart, you are, back from broken.

When you show love even when you
may not be loved, you are, back from broken.
When you can pick up the pieces and become
whole again, you are….

BACK FROM BROKEN

ABOUT THE AUTHOR

ROSHEKA SHONTA HENRY is a native of Georgia, and was raised in Alabama. She grew up to love the medical field, and spent the majority of her career working at surrounding community hospitals as a phlebotomist and patient register. She is a proud and devoted member of Word of Truth Ministries, where her father, Pastor John L. Cook is the Sr. Pastor. She is also a certified dance instructor, where she leads the dance ministry at her church. She also teaches praise dancing in the surrounding churches. Her praise dance ministry has been featured on local television stations numerous times.

She has received awards as well as trophies for her profound work in her dance ministry. She is very devoted to Kingdom work. God is her driving force. She is the author of **"BACK FROM BROKEN...A DANCERS JOURNEY BACK TO WHOLENESS"**, which is the autobiography of her life. She has written a gospel song called **"Hallelujah"** song by an up and coming artist, that can be downloaded on all major online music apps, such as iTunes and Google Play. She is also a single mother of three gifted children.

Her passion in life is to empower women, as well as men, and children. Her love for mankind has driven her to pursue a path that will inspire others to be all that they can be in life and in Christ. She is an Motivational speaker as well as an advocate for women who are broken. She works closely with her church and local food bank feeding the hungry.

Rosheka has also had the opportunity to model for The Wonderful World of Fashion Show. She has been known to grace the camera with her smile for multiple companies in her area. She has a bright future in ministry and is looking to open a Non-profit Organization **THE BACK FROM BROKEN LLC.CENTER** for broken women/men looking to get back to wholeness.

To connect with the author for speaking engagements, conferences or appearances you can contact her through the following ways

Website: www.backfrombroken.com

Email: rosheka.henry@gmail.com

www.facebook.com/backfrombroken

Instagram: @backfrombroken1

Twitter: @backfrombroken